THE
LITTLE
BOOK
OF
WARWICKSHIRE

THE
LITTLE
BOOK
OF
WARWICKSHIRE

LYNNE R. WILLIAMS

The
History
Press

First published 2015

The History Press
The Mill, Brimscombe Port
Stroud, Gloucestershire, GL5 2QG
www.thehistorypress.co.uk

British Library Cataloguing in Publication Data.
A catalogue record for this book is available from the British Library.

ISBN 978 0 7509 5372 6

Typesetting and origination by Thomas Bohm, User Design,
Illustration and Typesetting
Printed and bound in Great Britain by TJ International Ltd.

CONTENTS

ACKNOWLEDGEMENTS

I would like to thank the following for their valuable contributions and especially my husband, Paul, for his enthusiasm and support.

Paul Williams; Matt Williams; Peter Lee (Nuneaton History Society); Warwickshire Museum; Dee Hawke; Tony Edlin; Keith Higginson; Leamington Spa Art Gallery and Museum.

Author illustrations appear on pages 17, 18, 20, 26, 28, 59, 151 and 165. All other images are copyright of The History Press.

INTRODUCTION

Well I didn't know that! Whether you want to delve into the history, geography, topography, ecology and personalities of Warwickshire or just dip in for a fun read, this quirky little book has it all!

Leafy Warwickshire reveals a wealth of fascinating facts, with plenty of heroes and villains, folklore and history thrown in along the way. A lurid past of dastardly deeds and martyrdom is also uncovered, where executions took the form of beheading, burning and hanging and, in the case of 'wicked Loddy', being pressed to death with stones.

Although landlocked, Warwickshire is blessed with an abundance of waterways that enabled many industries to flourish in the mid-eighteenth century. Cottage industries such as weaving, hatting, clock, watch and needle making became factory based and thrived with waterwheels driving the machinery. The building of canals enabled transportation of heavy goods and cheap coal from the coalfields in the north of the county and many more industries were established. This gave rise to a substantial increase in the population.

Towns have been built by quarrying the local stone and excavations have revealed exciting discoveries such as Neolithic, Saxon and Roman remains, which tell stories of how these societies were organised and how they lived their everyday lives. Prehistoric giants such as the skeleton of the Honington plesiosaur have also been unearthed and now repose in the Warwick Museum. Earthworks and ruins of motte and bailey castles are peppered throughout Warwickshire, recorded in Domesday in 1086, and evidence of Neolithic burial grounds remain. All weave a rich tapestry of the county's ancient past that, thanks to modern archaeological techniques, can be preserved in the present.

From medieval times to modernity, customs have played a part in the everyday lives of the townsfolk and village folk. Every Shrove Tuesday the 800-year-old custom of the Atherstone Ball Game is played in the streets and is akin to running with the bulls at Pamplona, while in October the equally ancient custom of the Mop Fair is held in Stratford-upon-Avon and Warwick. The old Court Leets still continue in Henley-in-Arden and Alcester and morris dancing, which once entertained Elizabeth I at Kenilworth Castle, regularly features at festivals. More recently other customs have been established, such as Carols at the Castle in December, the Victorian Fair in November and Apple Wassailing at Ryton Organic Gardens. The Sealed Knot re-enact battles that took place in Warwickshire, notably the Battle of Edgehill which, in 1642, was the first major battle of the English Civil War and ended in a bloody stalemate with over 3,000 bodies strewn between Radway and Kineton in what became known as the 'Red Row'.

Education has long been important in the area. Warwick School can claim a heritage that reaches as far back as 1042 and Edward the Confessor, and possibly further. It then became a grammar school under the endowment of Henry VIII. Charity schools known as Bluecoat schools were the forerunner of today's public schools and taught poor scholars basic reading, writing and arithmetic, the most famous being Rugby School, which was popularised in Thomas Hughes' *Tom Brown's Schooldays*.

Home to Shakespeare and other great poets and writers, Warwickshire has been a source of inspiration. From the Great Forest of Arden, with its coalfields and the arable Feldon area to the south separated by the lovely River Avon, the beauty of the county is revealed with its open country parks, gentle rolling countryside, graceful waterways, historic towns and stately homes. The hustle and bustle of its industrial past can also still be seen with the preservation of mills, watermills and factory buildings.

The Little Book of Warwickshire is an eclectic compilation and a voyage of discovery that will enlighten, educate, amaze, astound, horrify and amuse; providing a great source of fun facts and quiz material.

Lynne R. Williams
2015

1

LOCALITIES AND LANDMARKS

PLACE NAMES AND THEIR ORIGINS

Domesday Book – compiled for William the Conqueror in 1086 to establish how much money could be raised in taxes – was an extensive land survey designed to assess the extent of land and resources and who owned it.

Ten Warwickshire place names recorded in Domesday and their Anglo-Saxon meanings:

Atherstone	*Aderestone*	Farmstead or village of a man called Aethelred
Barford	*Bereforde*	A ford or river crossing for conveying barley
Chilvers Coton	*Celverdestoche*	Ceolfrith's Cottage
Dunchurch	*Donecerce*	The church on the hill
Kenilworth	*Chinewrde*	Farm of a woman
Hartshill	*Andreshille*	Heardred's Hill
Luddington	*Luditone*	Luda's farm
Shipston	*Scepwestun*	Sheep wash town
Tysoe	*Tikeshoche*	Spur of land dedicated to the God Tiw
Ullenhall	*Ulverlei*	Nook or piece of land

A reference to Warwickshire first appears in 1001 as *Waeringscir*, meaning 'dwellings by the weir'.

Warwick was the only town in the County of Warwickshire in 1066.

The County of Warwickshire is divided into five districts: North Warwickshire, Nuneaton and Bedworth, Rugby, Warwick, and Stratford-upon-Avon.

The boundaries, which historically encompassed Coventry and much of Birmingham, were set in the local government reorganisation of 1974.

In the seventeenth century, Warwickshire was divided into hundreds, which were the territorial and legal divisions. Each hundred had its own court. These were the Knightlow hundred, Kineton hundred, Barlichway hundred and Hemlingford hundred.

Leafy Warwickshire was once home to the Forest of Arden, a great forested area to the north-west of the River Avon. By the 1600s much of this forest had been cleared as the land was given over to arable and sheep farming, which had become staple industries. In 1895 woodland covered about 21,000 acres, including recent plantations. By 1985 only 6,000 acres remained as semi-natural woodland. Many of the village names in the Arden ended in 'ley', which signified a clearing in the wood.

In the 1960s there were still thousands of elm trees throughout the county, often attaining heights of 60–80ft and helping to create 'leafy Warwickshire'. However, in the 1970s and early '80s, Dutch elm disease spread throughout the county and necessitated the felling of nearly all of Warwickshire's mature elms. Today only two trees of any significance remain, one outside Wellesbourne and the other in the area of Alcester.

Warwickshire was divided into two sections, the cultivated Feldon south of the River Avon and the Great Forest of Arden bounded by the Roman roads, Icknield Street and Watling Street. In 1540, John Leland wrote: 'The ground in Arden is muche enclosyd, plentifull of gres but no great plenty of corne. The other part of Warwykshire that lyeth on the left hond or ripe of Avon river, muche to the southe, is for the most part champion, somewhat barren of wood, but very plentifull of corne.'

The largest English oak in the Arden can be found at Stoneleigh Abbey and measures 9.2m around its circumference. It is said to be 1,000 years old.

TEN UNUSUAL PLACE NAMES FROM WARWICKSHIRE

Bermuda Place: Suburb of Nuneaton
Boot Hill: Grendon, Atherstone, north Warwickshire

Chickabiddy Lane: Southam
Copdock Hill: Hampton Lucy
Cut Throat Lane: Tanworth-in-Arden
Foul End: Near Water Orton, north Warwickshire
Squab Hall: Bishops Tachbrook, near Royal Leamington Spa
Tink-a-Tank: Warwick
Wheelbarrow Castle: Grade II listed building, Barton-on-the-Heath
Wiggerland Wood: Grade II listed building, Bishops Tachbrook

WARWICKSHIRE RHYME

A famous Warwickshire rhyme characterised certain villages:

Piping Pebworth, Dancing Marston
Haunted Hillboro', Hungry Grafton
Dodging Exhall, Papist Wixford
Beggarly Broom and Drunkard Bidford

POPULATION

The largest towns in Warwickshire (using population figures given in 2004) are:
Nuneaton (population 77,500)
Rugby (population 62,700)
Leamington Spa (population 45,300)
Bedworth (population 32,500)

PARISHES

Ten Parishes in the Arden
Population figures according to the 2001 census.

Baddesley Clinton: Population 190. The moated manor house was once owned by Nicholas Brome, who murdered the parish priest when he caught him chucking his wife under the chin. Pardoned by the king for his crimes, Nicholas sought to make amends by building the church at Baddesley Clinton and leaving instructions that on his death he be buried upright at the church door so that everyone entering should step on him. He died in 1517.

Baddesley Ensor: Population 1,921. A former mining village, the Roman road of Watling Street forms the boundary of the parish at its north-east angle for approximately 300yds. It is known for its common with beautiful views looking towards Birmingham, Leicestershire, Derbyshire and Staffordshire.

Bearley: Population 758. Home to Bearley Vineyard, which was established in 2005 and is the winner of numerous regional and national awards for wines.

Fillongley: Population 3,393. In medieval times there were two castles here.

Hampton-in-Arden: Population 1,787. The parish church of St Mary and St Bartholomew has an unusual north doorway near the west end.

Haseley: Population 207. The old manor house, dated 1561, was built by Clement Throckmorton.

Henley-in-Arden: Population 2,011. Market town, originally a hamlet of Wootton Wawen.

Lapworth: Population 2,100. This parish includes two National Trust sites: Baddesley Clinton, a moated manor house, and Packwood House.

Stoneleigh: Population 2,781. A small village on the River Sowe. To the south-west of the village is Stoneleigh Abbey, founded by the Cistercian monks in 1154 and owned by the Leigh family from 1561–1990.

Temple Balsall: Population 6,234, including inhabitants of Fen End and Chadwick End. Once the headquarters of the Templars. A hamlet in the Metropolitan Borough of Solihull, formerly in Warwickshire.

In contrast to the heavily wooded and sparsely populated area of the Arden, the open countryside of the Feldon or Fielden with its compact villages was more densely populated.

Ten Parishes in the Feldon Area
Population figures according to the 2001 census.

Barford: Population 1,171. Birthplace of Joseph Arch who is credited with the formation of the National Agricultural Labourers Union in 1872. Also home to super centenarian Annie Butler, who was 112 years old when she died in 2009 and retains second place in the list of oldest people to have lived in the United Kingdom.

Charlecote: Population 226. Small village on the River Avon. Charlecote Manor is a National Trust property with a deer park. The park was laid out by Lancelot 'Capability' Brown.

Combrook: Population (see Kineton). Combrook was formerly a 'closed' village entirely owned by the Lord of the Manor until the sale of Compton Verney estate in 1929. It is considered to be one of the best-preserved estate villages in the country.

Fenny Compton: Population 797. Although a small village it supported two railway stations, that of the Great Western Railway and the Stratford and Midland Junction Railway.

Gaydon: Population 376. The Gaydon Inn was once famous for its association with highwaymen. John Smith was arrested for a hold-up at the inn and was later hanged at Warwick.

Great Wolford: Population 203. To the west of the village is Wolford Wood, an ancient woodland designated a Site of Special Scientific Interest in 1987.

Kineton: Population 2,278 (including Combrook). At the foot of Pittern Hill are the remains of the earthworks of a motte and bailey castle known as St John's Castle.

Priors Marston: Population 506. Home to a disused Moravian chapel in Keyes Lane.

Radway: Population 259. The church of St Peter houses the effigy of Captain Henry Kingsmill who fought for Charles I and was killed at the Battle of Edgehill in 1642.

Whatcote: Population 153. Whatcote was one of the last places in the country to practice 'rough music', where the villagers drove an unmarried couple away, banging metal objects together and burning effigies of the pair.

SHELDON TAPESTRY

Warwick Museum houses the famous Sheldon Tapestry Map of Warwickshire. The tapestry was woven in the hamlet of Barcheston in the sixteenth century (possibly 1588) and measures 13ft high by 18ft wide. It is one of a set of four commissioned by wealthy landowner Ralph Sheldon to hang in his newly built house at Weston near Long Compton. After spending some time on loan to the Victoria & Albert Museum in London, it was purchased by the Warwickshire Museum in 1960.

The Sheldon Tapestry is a graphic record of William Shakespeare's Elizabethan England and depicts the hills, rivers, open fields, forests, towns, villages and great houses of the gentry. It carries the following inscription: 'Warwickshire, so named as well of the Saxons as of us at this daye; it is divided into two parts by the river Avone running through the midest. The one is called Feldon, the other woodland.'

The Sheldon Tapestry is the pictorial forerunner of the Ordnance Survey maps.

MOTORWAYS

Warwickshire is served by six motorways:
The M40 connects Birmingham with London and runs through the centre of the county, serving Leamington Spa, Warwick and Stratford.
   The M6 connects the north-west and West Midlands to the M1 and runs through the north of Warwickshire, serving Rugby, Nuneaton and Bedworth on its way to Birmingham.
   The M69 from Coventry to Leicester serves Nuneaton.
   Other motorways that pass briefly through Warwickshire include the M45, a short spur south of Rugby connecting with the M1, the southern end of the M6 Toll and the M42, which passes through Warwickshire at several points.

BOUNDARY

The Fosse forms a boundary to parishes for 29 of the 40 miles it runs from High Cross, Leicester in the north-east to Cirencester in the south-west, much of this distance across Warwickshire.

BURIED TREASURE

Meon Hill was once the site of an Iron Age hill fort in 700 BC–AD 43.

The largest hoard of early Roman coins so far found in the West Midlands was discovered on Edge Hill in 2008. Buried for over 1,900 years and dating from when the Romans ruled in Britain, the hoard found in a small pot contained 1,146 silver Denari coins. The last coin to be added to the collection depicted the head of Emperor Nero.

Manduessum (the Roman name for Mancetter) was the major location of Roman pottery producers who occupied the site for 400 years.

In 1922, a large Anglo-Saxon burial ground was discovered in Bidford-upon-Avon and a hoard of jewels, shields and other artefacts were revealed dating back to AD 500.

CASTLES IN THE AIR

Warwickshire was once peppered with Norman motte and bailey castles, many of which have either disappeared leaving nothing more than earthworks as evidence. Others were timber-built but gradually replaced with stone and these remain as partially excavated ruins.

A sixteenth-century timber-framed building referred to as the 'old castle manor' stands on the site once occupied by Studley Castle built in the eleventh century by William Courbucion.

Earthworks are all that remain of the former Norman motte and bailey Beaudesert Castle in Henley-in-Arden. Originally the castle was surrounded by a deep dry moat and would have been built of timber but gradually replaced with stone. A dig was carried out by the BBC's *Time Team* in September 2001 and their findings suggested that the castle would originally have been a large hall with a solar.

Allesley Castle may have been erected by Lord Hastings in the early fourteenth century and the medieval ringwork survives as earthworks. The castle mound is a substantial circular earthworks motte measuring 50m in diameter and surrounded by a dry ditch moat.

At Astley Castle a moat, a gateway and curtain walls survive the fortified manor house built in 1226. The manor was acquired by the Grey family in 1450 but in 1461 Sir John Grey was killed fighting for the Lancastrians at St Albans, leaving a widow, Elizabeth Woodville, who then married Edward IV. The castle later became the home of Sir Henry Grey, Duke of Suffolk, and his daughter, Lady Jane Grey, who ruled as queen for nine days. When Lady Jane Grey and her father were beheaded at the Tower of London in 1554 the manor was demolished on the orders of Mary Tudor but rebuilt by Sir Henry's widow. In 1654 the Newdigate family of Arbury acquired the estate and in 1820 Gothic additions were made. Now owned by the Landmark Trust, the red sandstone building, with its embattled parapets, is now a holiday let built within the ruins.

Bagot's Castle in Baginton is a fourteenth-century castle rebuilt by Sir William Bagot in the late 1300s. The original building is believed to have been constructed in the eleventh century during the reign of Henry I. In the seventeenth century the castle was replaced with a hall and was the seat of the Bromley family from 1698. The house was destroyed by fire in 1889 and excavation work carried out in the twentieth century exposed the remains of the castle.

Brailes Castle, which dates from the mid-twelfth century, was probably constructed by Roger de Beaumont, Earl of Warwick. Earthworks remain of the Norman motte and bailey.

Churchover Castle is described by *The Gatehouse Record* as being a well-preserved little moated mount castle. The earthwork motte founded by the Waure family in the eleventh century is surrounded by a wet ditch.

The ruins of Fillongley Castle, built by the Hastings family in the twelfth century, are situated at Castle Yard. It was turned into a fortified manor house at the start of the fourteenth century and left to decay in the fifteenth century. An earlier motte castle known as 'Old Fillongley' on Castle Hills was abandoned in the thirteenth century.

By the River Stour in Halford are the earthworks and buried remains of Halford Castle, thought to have been in use in the fourteenth century. A low mound of the motte standing 4m high can be found in the grounds of Halford Manor, which replaced it.

Hartshill Castle was built by Hugh de Hadreshill in the twelfth century. On top of the motte was a wooden tower that served to house the Lord of the Manor and his family as well as being a lookout tower. A Tudor house was built in 1560 incorporating the bailey walls of the castle but was demolished in the 1950s.

Seckington Castle, a motte and bailey built in the eleventh century by the Earl of Meulan, is a conical motte measuring 9m high and 46m in diameter. The castle is protected as a Scheduled Ancient Monument since 1923 and is on the edge of the village, surrounded on three sides by traces of ridge and furrow cultivation.

The motte and bailey at Brinklow was the largest in Warwickshire with the motte standing 12.192m high and 18.288m wide and the bailey extending 121.92m x 152.4m.

CASTLES STANDING

The town of Warwick is home to what has been described as the finest surviving medieval castle in the country, albeit with embellishments and additions made in the seventeenth, eighteenth and nineteenth centuries.

From its beginnings in the eleventh century, the Norman motte and bailey moated castle has been the seat of the earls of Warwick and continued as such for many centuries.

Originally a timber-built structure dating from the time of William the Conqueror in 1068, the castle was replaced with stone. Ethelfleda's Mound, which still exists to the present day, was said to be the first fortification on the site in 914.

Warwick Castle was sold to Madame Tussauds in 1978 and taken over by America's biggest theme park company, Merlin Entertainments, in 2007. It is now one of the United Kingdom's biggest tourist attractions.

Guy and Caesars Towers were constructed in the fourteenth century and formed part of a formidable set of defences. Bear and Clarence Towers represent the remains of a fifteenth-century fortification and Bear Tower is so called because it had a bear pit and was used for bear baiting. The Bear Tower was investigated by Tony Robinson from BBC's *Time Team* on 15 February 2013.

Maxstoke Castle is a fine example of a moated and fortified manor house that has survived largely intact. Commissioned by William de

Clinton, 1st Earl of Huntingdon, in 1345, additions were made by
Humphrey Stafford, Duke of Buckingham, who acquired the castle in
1437. A Grade I listed building and Scheduled Ancient Monument, it
is in private ownership but opens to the public on occasion. Maxstoke
has been in the continuous ownership of the Dilke (later Fetherston
Dilke) families since the seventeenth century.

The substantial ruins of Kenilworth Castle, described by architectural
historian Anthony Emery as 'the finest surviving example of a semi-
royal palace of the later Middle Ages, significant for its scale, form
and quality of workmanship', was once the seat of Robert Dudley,
Earl of Leicester. Originally founded in the 1100s around a Norman
great tower, it was enlarged by King John at the beginning of the
thirteenth century. Robert Dudley constructed new buildings in
which to entertain and impress Elizabeth I on her visits to the castle,
particularly her final visit in 1575.

True to form, the Parliamentarians slighted the castle to prevent it from becoming a Royalist stronghold. Then in 1650 Parliamentarian Colonel Hawksworth acquired the castle and converted Dudley's gatehouse into a residence for himself.

The Great Mere, which was once filled with water and provided protection for the castle, has long since been drained and is now meadowland.

The Grade I Scheduled Ancient Monument has been managed by English Heritage since 1984 and is open to the public. Elizabeth I's bedchamber was made accessible to the public in September 2014.

RELIGIOUS STRUCTURES AND BURIAL PLACES

Cursuses are long parallel banks of earth that linked various religious monuments in the Neolithic period and were used for special processions during burial ceremonies. Evidence of these has been found at Charlecote, Barford Sheds and Longbridge, Warwick. Corpses were taken to mortuary enclosures before burial.

The henge, a Neolithic earthwork featuring a ring bank and ditch inside the bank, which was used for meeting places for religious ceremony, was discovered at Sherbourne near Warwick.

The only surviving henge monument in Warwickshire is the Rollright Stones that stand on the Cotswold border with Oxfordshire.

It has been suggested that Mancetter in north Warwickshire is possibly the site of the last battle of Boudica, leader of the Iceni tribe, against the Romans in AD 60–61.

Evidence of a long barrow, a massive earth mound covering burial chambers, was found at Wasperton near Warwick.

The church in Henley-in-Arden is dedicated to St Nicholas and his image is depicted on the weather vane on the tower of the church. St Nicholas was a fourth-century Greek Christian who was venerated for his compassion and help for the poor, sick and needy, and especially as the protector of children and sailors. He became Bishop of Myra but, under the persecution of Christians by Diocletian, he was exiled and imprisoned. The anniversary of his death, on 6 December AD 343 (19 December in the Julian calendar), became a day of celebration. Today St Nicholas is better known as Santa Claus.

The oldest church in Warwickshire is St Peter's in Wootton Wawen. The church, possibly 1,100 years old, houses a Saxon sanctuary. A semi-circular stained-glass memorial window tells the story of St Kenelm, a 7-year-old boy who succeeded his father to the throne of Mercia but was then murdered by order of his aunt.

A stone monument surmounted with a cross stands in the wood on Blacklow Hill, Warwick, and commemorates the execution of Piers Gaveston, Earl of Cornwall. The plaque reads: 'Here in this hollow was beheaded on 1st day of July 1312, Piers Gaveston, Earl of Cornwall, killed by barons lawless as himself, the minion of a hateful king, in life and in death, a memorable instance of misrule.' The monument was erected by Bertie Greatheed, squire of Guy's Cliffe Manor in 1821.

The first Roman temple to be found in Warwickshire was excavated in the late 1970s at Grimstock Hill near Coleshill.

The thirteenth-century church of St Peter and St Paul at Coleshill houses an unusual effigy. In the floor of the chancel lies a brass figure of the first vicar of the Reformation, John Fenton, whose right hand displays five fingers and a thumb.

An eighteenth-century record breaker, Thomas Spooner is buried in the churchyard of St Matthews at Shuttington. Thomas' claim to fame was as the fattest man in England, weighing 40 stone 9lbs and measuring 4ft 3in across his shoulders.

An unusual headstone graces the churchyard of St Lawrence's in Oxhill. It is inscribed: 'Here lyeth the body of Myrtilla, negro slave to Mr Tho. Beauchamp of Nevis. Bapd. Oct. Ye 20th and buried Jan. 6th 1705.'

In *Antiquities of Warwickshire*, William Dugdale lists the collection of relics once held in St Mary's church, Warwick, as recorded in 1455. These included fragments of the True Cross, various relics of the Virgin Mary, and the bones and other remains of more than thirty saints. There was also the ivory horn of St George, a stone on which his blood fell when he was martyred and a piece of the burning bush that Moses saw.

A memorial window at the church of St Peter in Binton depicts the expedition of Captain Robert Scott to the South Pole, which commenced in 1910.

Windows in the church of St Denis, Little Compton, depict the execution and burial of Charles I on 30 January 1649. He is accompanied by his chaplain, William Juxon, Bishop of London. Juxon became Archbishop of Canterbury and later crowned Charles' son, Charles II, in Westminster Abbey. He retired to Little Compton.

TEN PLACES OF INTEREST

Chilvers Coton Heritage Centre: This collection revolves around memories from past communities to present.

Compton Verney Art Gallery: Located near Kineton, this eighteenth-century Grade I country mansion is set in 120 acres of landscaped parkland designed by Capability Brown. Collections include Neapolitan art 1600–1800, North European medieval art 1450–1650 and Chinese bronzes.

Coventry Transport Museum: Located in Millennium Place, this is one of the largest attractions of its kind in Europe. Notable exhibits are Thrust2 and ThrustSSC, the British jet cars that broke the land speed record in 1983 and 1997.

Herbert Art Gallery & Museum: Located at Jordon Well, Coventry, collections include sculpture, old masters paintings, art since 1900 and local history. There is also a cafe area and education, training, creative media and arts information facilities.

Heritage Motor Centre Museum: The world's greatest collection of classic, vintage and veteran British cars. This museum can be found on Banbury Road, Gaydon.

Leamington Art Gallery & Museum: This award-winning gallery at the Royal Pump Rooms houses over 11,000 objects in the fields of art, crafts, sculpture, local and social history, archaeology and ethnography.

Mechanical, Art & Design (MAD) Museum: Located in Sheep Street, Stratford-upon-Avon, this museum displays an exciting collection of machinery, incorporating gears, chains, pulleys and whirligigs. It is an extravaganza of automata and kinetic art.

Nuneaton Museum & Art Gallery: Collections include fine and decorative art, social and industrial history, and objects from the life and times of both novelist George Eliot and television comedian and game show host, Larry Grayson.

St John's Museum, Warwick: The museum includes a Victorian schoolroom and kitchen, and houses costumes and memorabilia of the Warwickshire Fusiliers.

The Webb Ellis Rugby Football Museum: Situated in Rugby town centre, the memorabilia includes a Gilbert football first exhibited at the Great Exhibition in London and an original Richard Lindon brass hand pump. Traditional rugby balls are still made at the museum.

NATIONAL TRUST PROPERTIES

Warwickshire boasts six National Trust properties and a rare fourteenth-century circular dovecote at Kinwarton near Alcester with 1m-thick walls, hundreds of nesting holes and an original rotating ladder. The properties are as follows:

Baddesley Clinton: Grade I listed moated manor house originally owned by John Brome and later home to the Ferrers family.

Charlecote Park: Grade I listed building with grounds sculptured by Capability Brown. Home to the Lucy family, followed by the Fairfax family.

Coughton Court: Grade I listed Tudor building (pronounced 'coat-un'). It was implicated in the Gunpowder Plot of 1605 and is home to the Throckmortons.

Farnborough Hall: Grade I listed building, home to the Holbech family.

Packwood House: Grade I listed Tudor building owned by John Fetherston and later Graham Baron Ash. It was donated to the National Trust in 1941.

Upton House: Built by Sir Rushout Cullen in 1695, it was then owned by banker Francis Child and George Child Villiers of the Jersey family and later the Bearsted family. Marcus Bearsted was famously the founder of the oil company Shell Transport and Trading.

SPA TOWN

The first brick of the first house to be built in New Town, Leamington Spa, was laid on 8 October 1808 by George Stanley, a Warwick stonemason.

The Pump Room baths were opened in 1814 at a cost of nearly £30,000. Although the saline springs of Leamington Priors, as it was then called, had been recognised as early as 1586, it wasn't until the arrival of Benjamin Satchwell in 1787 that they became exploited. By the early nineteenth century, several baths had been established and the town was now called Leamington Spa. A common warm or hot bath cost 2*s* 6*d*, a marble bath 3*s* and a cold bath 1*s*. At the new baths the charge for a warm bath was 3*s* and a cold bath 1*s* 6*d*. Queen Victoria visited the town in 1838 and gave her permission to call it Royal Leamington Spa.

The Regent Hotel was opened in 1819. First known as 'William's Hotel' the title was changed to Regent by permission of George IV who visited it. It was closed in 1998 but reopened in 2003 as a Travelodge after refurbishment.

TEN WARWICKSHIRE WINDMILLS

Burton Dassett Mill: Built in 1664, it ceased working around 1912.

Chesterton: Grade I listed tower mill of unique design with an arched base. This windmill was built for Parliamentarian Sir Edward Peyto in 1632 and ceased working in 1910. It was restored by Warwickshire County Council in 1965–71.

Napton Windmill: Built around 1835, it ceased working by sails in around 1900 and by steam in around 1909.

Norton Lindsey Tower Mill: Built in the Imperial period, steam was added in 1889 and it last worked in 1906. The mill is now undergoing restoration.

Rowington Tower Mill: Called 'Bouncing Bess' the mill was used as a prisoner-of-war dormitory during the First World War and converted into a house in 1978.

Shrewley disused wooden-post windmill: Formerly called 'Pinchem', this windmill was originally built in Claverdon in 1803 and was moved to Shrewley Common in 1832.

Southam 'Old Mill': Built in around 1807, the mill was rebuilt after a fire in 1849 and demolished in the early 1980s.

Stockton Post Windmill: Built in 1810, it ceased work in 1879 and was demolished in 1923.

Thurlaston Tower Mill: Built in 1794, it was last used in 1910 and collapsed in 1937.

Upper Tysoe Tower Mill: Restored with metal-roofed cap in March 2004. The sails have gone and only the stocks remain.

WATERMILLS

The use of water power was instrumental in establishing industries during the Industrial Revolution in the mid-eighteenth century and waterwheels were used for fulling mills and grinding corn. The introduction of steam power allowed manufacturing industries to flourish when the textiles industries declined. Warwickshire watermills that are still in existence (mainly for educative purposes and as attractions rather than for production) include:

Arrow Mill   Alcester
Hotel with waterwheel in restaurant

Charlecote Mill   Hampton Lucy
A working mill producing traditionally stone-ground flours through French burr stones and open on occasion to visitors

The Saxon Mill   Warwick
Waterwheel and restaurant

Wellesbourne Water Mill
Coffee shop, art and craft barn and waterwheel that operated commercially until 1958

CHOCKS AWAY

By the end of the Second World War over 600 military airfields had been established in Great Britain, including seventeen in Warwickshire. These seventeen airfields used by the Royal Air Force during the Second World War were:

Ansty: January 1940–March 1953. A training base for RAF pilots until 1944, it closed in 1953.

Atherstone-on-Stour: April 1941–November 1945. Located 3.5 miles south of Stratford-upon-Avon. Satellite for Wellesbourne Mountford and Pershore.

Baginton: September 1940–45. Used as a municipal airfield since 1930.

Bramcote: June 1940–November 1946. Used as a training base for instructors, it was closed in 1946 by the RAF and transferred to the Fleet Air Arm in December 1946 when it became HMS Gamecock.

Brinklow: October 1941–December 1945. Satellite landing ground used for storage and repair of aircraft.

Castle Bromwich: 1926–April 1958. Allocated to the Army Co-operation Command for training anti-aircraft and searchlight crews.

Church Lawford: May 1941–55. Training base for instructors.

Elmdon: May 1939–February 1946. Flying training school.

Gaydon: June 1942–December 1974. Main role as a Wellington bomber crew training station.

Hockley Heath: December 1941–December 1945. Relief landing ground for Elmdon and Church Lawford.

Honiley: May 1941–March 1958. Main role as a night fighter station.

Leamington Spa: December 1941–December 1945. Located 3 miles south of Leamington Spa. Grass landing strip.

Long Marston: November 1941–54. Satellite for RAF Honeybourne.

Snitterfield: March 1943–46. Flying training school and satellite for Church Lawford.

Southam: June 1940–December 1945. Relief landing ground for Ansty and Church Lawford.

Warwick: December 1941–45. Located off the Stratford Road south of Warwick. Relief landing ground for Church Lawford.

Wellesbourne Mountford: April 1941–63. Main role as a Wellington bomber crew training station.

Airfields Currently in Use
Baginton: Now Coventry Airport.

Elmdon: Birmingham Airport.

Long Marston: Used by flying clubs and microlights.

Snitterfield: Now Stratford Gliding Club.

Wellesbourne Mountford: Wellesbourne Airfield used by flying clubs and helicopters.

2

NATURAL HISTORY

GEOLOGY OF WARWICKSHIRE

Rocks from the Permian, Triassic, Jurassic and Carboniferous periods dominate much of Warwickshire.

The oldest rocks belong to the Precambrian Period and are about 600 million years old. Warwickshire in the Precambrian and Cambrian periods was characterised by volcanoes and later by extensive seas.

Purley Quarry at Mancetter provides a rare opportunity to view some of the oldest rocks in the Midlands.

The Cambrian period of 350 million years ago is represented by a prominent ridge running north-west from Nuneaton towards Atherstone.

Beneath the former Forest of Arden in the north of the county are red clays and sandstones of the Mercia Mudstone, also called Keuper Marl, Keuper Red Sandstone and Arden Sandstone, while the south is characterised by Lias clays.

The Warwickshire coalfields prevalent in the north were brought about by the older Carboniferous rocks pushing up through the Mercia Mudstone and eroding it.

The cave of the romantic hero turned hermit, Guy of Guy's Cliffe, Warwick, was cut from the soft Triassic sandstone.

The largest landfill site in Europe is located near to Packington in north Warwickshire and covers 160 hectares (400 acres).

The highest point in Warwickshire is Ilmington Downs at 242m.

Warwickshire Nature Conservation Trust was founded in 1970 as a registered charity.

FOREST OF ARDEN

The Forest of Arden covered an area stretching from Stratford-upon-Avon in the south to Tamworth in the north of the county and included Birmingham and Coventry.

No Roman roads were built through the forest; however, it was bounded by the Roman roads Icknield Street, Watling Street, Fosse Way and a prehistoric salt track leading from Droitwich.

By 1086, in the time of Domesday, about 35 per cent of north Warwickshire is known to have been wooded. Much of the forest was cleared during the Middle Ages.

The dominant tree in the Arden area is oak.

Place names ending in 'ley' signified the settlement originated as a woodland clearing, e.g. Henley-in-Arden, Bearley, Oversley and Fillongley.

The Knights Templar owned a preceptory at Temple Balsall in the middle of the Forest of Arden from 1162 to 1312. It was then passed to the Knights Hospitallers until the Reformation in the sixteenth century.

Robert Catesby, leader of the Gunpowder Plot in 1605, was a native of Lapworth, a village in the Arden.

Shakespeare's play *As You Like It* is set in the Forest of Arden and was an adaptation of an earlier play by Thomas Lodge originally set in French woodlands.

An ancient stone known as 'Coughton Cross' is located at the southern end of Coughton Court owned by the National Trust.

'SEA DRAGON'

During the nineteenth century the early Jurassic limestone of south-east Warwickshire was quarried for flooring, gravestones, walling and for making lime and cement. When quarrying was being carried out at Wilmcote Quarry, the skeleton of a magnificent 'sea-dragon', the plesiosaur, was discovered. This crocodile-like creature died out around 65–70 million years ago. The remains were donated to the Warwickshire Natural History and Archaeological Society in 1841 by the quarry owner, Richard Greaves.

Also discovered roughly 150 years ago was the Honington plesiosaur, which was found in the Lias clays of south Warwickshire and presented to the museum in 1866 by John William Kirshaw.

The fossilised remains of a 4.5m dinosaur, macroplata teniuceps, were discovered in a quarry in Bishops Itchington in 1927. The skeleton now resides in the Natural History Museum.

COUNTRY PARKS

Burton Dassett Hills near Gaydon/Kineton opened in 1971 and is a 100-acre series of rugged hilltops with spectacular panoramic views over the surrounding countryside. There is a prominent beacon, quarry remains and the twelfth-century All Saints' church nearby.

Ryton Pools near Ryton-on-Dunsmore covers 100 acres and provides different habitats for birds and wildlife.

Hartshill was opened in 1978 and covers 137 acres, including woodland and open hilltop with spectacular views across the Anker Valley.

Pooley, south of Shuttington and close to the M42, is 62.5 hectares, a third of which has been designated a Site of Special Scientific Interest. The park contains several pools and has a visitor centre and tearoom.

Kingsbury Water Park, previously the site of gravel extraction pits, encompasses fifteen lakes and over 600 acres of country park. Opened in May 1975, the park attracted 50,000 visitors during its first year. The many attractions include bird hides for observation of the many species that inhabit the lakes, a 7.25ft gauge ride on mini railway, model boat sailing, water sports and fishing. The lakes teem with roach, rudd, perch, carp, pike, bream and tench and plays host to the British Carp Championships.

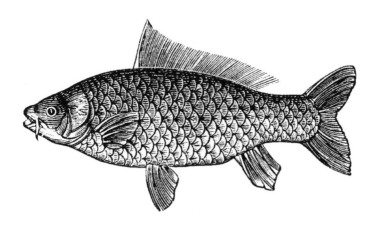

RESERVOIRS

Draycote reservoir was built between 1967–69 on what was previously agricultural land. It has a maximum depth of 70ft and holds a capacity of 5 billion gallons. The reservoir covers 630 acres and there is a 5-mile path around its edge for walkers and cyclists.

Draycote is home to a variety of wildlife and is nationally important for a species of duck, the smew, while being regionally important for golden eye and goosander as well. The species of birds that can be observed include: scaup; common scoter and slovian and black-necked grebes; glaucos, Iceland, Mediterranean and little gulls. Migrants in spring and autumn are black and Arctic terns and osprey. The reservoir is also home to all three common species of wagtails and kingfishers.

Shustoke Reservoir is 400m at its widest point. The River Bourne feeds the smaller eastern pool (8 acres) and the water is then transferred to the main reservoir (92 acres). In the springtime there is an abundance of wildflowers, cowslips and lady's smock. The circuit around the main reservoir is 1.77 miles.

TEN WARWICKSHIRE RIVERS

Alne: A tributary of the River Arrow, which has its headwaters at Wootton Wawen.

Anker: Flows through the centre of Nuneaton towards Tamworth in Staffordshire.

Avon: Beginning in Naseby it flows through Welford-on-Avon, Rugby, Wolston, Warwick, Stratford-upon-Avon and Bidford-on-Avon.

Blythe: Flows through Warwickshire, from Solihull to Coleshill.

Dene: A tributary of the Avon, it merges at Charlecote Park. Its headwaters rise on the western slopes of Burton Dassett and flows towards Kineton.

Leam: Is a tributary of the River Avon and flows through rural Warwickshire, including Leamington Spa.

Sherbourne: Beginning at Corley, the Sherbourne merges into the Sowe at Baginton and ultimately into the Avon near Stoneleigh.

Sowe: A tributary of the Avon, which it joins at Stoneleigh from its source in Coventry.

Stour: A tributary of the Avon, which it joins at Stratford-upon-Avon, it flows through Halford, Alderminster, Newbold-on-Stour, Atherstone-on-Stour and Clifford Chambers.

Swift: A small clay-based tributary of the River Avon, it flows from Gilmorton in Leicestershire before joining the Avon at Rugby.

WATER, WATER EVERYWHERE

Royal Leamington Spa fared badly in the floods of 10 April 1998 and July 2007 when the River Leam burst its banks and deluged the centre of Leamington, flooding the Jephson Gardens, Pump Room Gardens and Welch's Meadow, effectively cutting the town in two.

Torrential rainfall in November 2012 saw schools shut, trains cancelled and roads closed across the whole of Warwickshire. Three elderly people had a lucky escape when their car was carried from a ford near Alcester and swept 450m down a swollen river before a farmer managed to stop it.

In the great Nuneaton flood of 1932 the water rose to 5ft high in the Market Place within an hour.

RARE AND LESS COMMON BUTTERFLIES

Some of the rarest species of butterflies inhabit the grassland sites of the Lias limestone quarries, particularly in the areas of Rugby and Harbury. Less common varieties are also to be found in various habitats in Warwickshire. Some of these include:

Dark Green Fritillary
Green-veined White
Grizzled Skipper
Holly Blue
Marbled White
Painted Lady
Small Heath
Small Skipper
The Small Blue Cupido
The Wall Lasiommata

SOCIAL BUMBLEBEES

Social bumblebees, prolific in Warwickshire up until the early twentieth century, went into decline. This was due to more intensive agriculture, which destroyed their flowering and open heathland natural habitats. More recently, two of the social species – the large garden bumblebee and brown-banded carder bee – are making a comeback, finding suitable habitats in the abandoned limestone quarries in south Warwickshire. Nature has re-established itself, providing Kidney Vetch and Bird's-foot Trefoil attracting bumblebees and butterflies alike. These sites are managed to protect their biodiversity.

Species of bumblebees found in Warwickshire include the common carder bee, the vestal cuckoo bee, Barbut's cuckoo bee, the hill cuckoo bee and field cuckoo bee.

RABBIT, RABBIT, RABBIT

The virulent disease myxomatosis was introduced in Warwickshire in 1956 and not only decimated the rabbit population but had the knock-on effect of bringing about a sharp decline in the number of buzzards who preyed on them. The disease was deliberately imported into the country from its origins in Australia to control the vast increase in the rabbit population.

DID YOU KNOW?

Meriden in Warwickshire is said to be the centre of England and a medieval cross marks the spot on the village green. The ancient wayside cross has been there for 500 years and was rebuilt on the site when the green was improved in celebration of the Festival of Britain in 1951. There is also a memorial to cyclists killed in action in the Second World War.

Upper, Middle and Lower Tysoe, below the escarpment of Edgehill, constitute the Vale of the Red Horse. The Red Horse was a giant figure that was originally carved into the red soil on the slopes of Edgehill. Its dimensions were 34ft from the crop to the chest, 14ft from ears to shoulder and 16ft from the shoulder to the ground. A nearby farm, called Red Horse Farm, was charged with the task of scouring the figure annually on Palm Sunday and the country folk who took part in the ceremony were usually regaled with cakes and ale. This custom gradually ceased and the figure eventually disappeared with enclosure of the open fields. It is thought that the figure was originally carved by Richard Neville, the 'Kingmaker', in honour of his charger, which he killed at the Battle of Towton to reassure his men he would not retreat from the battlefield.

Tattle Bank near Claverdon has been designated as a Site of Special Scientific Interest. Sandy gravel at the site is believed to have been formed during the Ice Age when two glaciers met along a line running north to south through Tattle Bank leaving behind boulders that cannot be matched with any stone known in Warwickshire. When the ice melted, a large lake known to geologists as Lake Harrison was formed before draining away to leave a fine muddy silt which today forms the fertile farming areas of Warwickshire.

A 9ft-high Russian brown or grizzly bear was shot in Alaska by one of the Dugdale family of Wroxall in 1883 and presented to the Warwickshire Natural History and Archaeology Society in 1912. The bear and ragged staff has been the emblem of Warwick earls for centuries.

The first humans to set foot in Warwickshire arrived a quarter of a million years ago.

Animals inhabiting Warwickshire in 125,000–70,000 BC included elephants, bears, hippos and lions.

Warwickshire boasts a total of 150 different species of slugs and snails compared with a national total of 200.

Some 29 per cent of the county is permanent grass farmland forming mainly pastures and meadows; 18 per cent is temporary leys-sown rye grass and clover for hay, silage and grazing; 2 per cent is laid to lawns, playing fields and golf courses; and 0.5 per cent is verges to roads and railways.

Warwickshire has 110 miles of canals and more than 1,700 miles of public rights of way and bridleways.

The record highest temperature is 35.7°C and was recorded at Stratford-upon-Avon in August 1990.

The lowest recorded temperature for Warwick is -17.8°C in January 1982.

3

LANDSCAPE AND HORTICULTURE

Garden design underwent radical changes, from the constrained planting within the rigid geometric patterns of knots and parterres in the sixteenth century to the sweeping open landscapes made popular by Capability Brown in the eighteenth century.

Having served an apprenticeship as a gardener on the Kirkharle estate in Northumberland, Capability first came to prominence as head gardener for Lord Cobham at Stowe, Buckinghamshire, when he was aged just 24 years. It was here that he developed the skills that were to lead to his acclaim as a leading landscape architect. Following the death of Lord Cobham, Capability struck out on his own, working on a freelance basis. He soon established a successful career pioneering his own inimitable style, which was to become his trademark and which he employed in stately homes throughout the country. Out went the constraints of the formal garden, with its boxed hedges and gravel pathways, and instead Capability introduced sweeping landscapes with lakes and clumps of trees to create a pleasing vista.

Knot gardens and parterres still form an integral part of the garden in many stately homes. The recreation of the Privy Garden at Kenilworth Castle is one such example.

A QUEEN'S PROGRESS

It was the custom of Elizabeth I to make a progress of the country during the summer months and visit some of her noblemen in their mansion houses. Over the years she made several journeys to Kenilworth Castle, seat of her favourite, Robert Dudley, Earl of Leicester. On her final visit in 1575, Dudley arranged a sumptuous pageant in her honour, greeting her with the Lady of the Lake rising out of the mere and symbolically relinquishing power over her domain to Elizabeth. Over the following days, Elizabeth was entertained with hunting, a particular passion of hers, punctuated with many songs, poems and pretty speeches. The visit culminated in a splendid fireworks display.

It was on this particular occasion that Dudley hoped to press his suit and persuade Elizabeth to marry him, and to this end he had spared no effort to please her. His *pièce d'résistance* was the creation of a beautiful Privy Garden especially for her. The intricate knot garden, abundantly planted with sweet-smelling flowers, herbs and fruit trees, was complemented with a magnificent centrepiece, an Atlas Fountain. This was described in a letter by Robert Laneham in the sixteenth century as 'a very fair fountain cast into an eight square, reared a four foot high; from the midst whereof a column up set in shape of two Athlants jointed together a back half. The water cascaded from the globe into the basin wherein pleasantly playing to and fro and round about, carp, tench, bream and, for variety, perch and eel.' Also in the garden was an aviary that Laneham described as being much beautified with diamonds and jewels.

Following Dudley's death in 1588 the garden was simplified and laid out as a parterre. In 1984 English Heritage took on the care and maintenance of the castle and ambitiously decided to recreate the Privy Garden as it would have been seen by Elizabeth. In order to accomplish this, much groundwork needed to be done and the services of experts were employed. Brian Dix, an experienced archaeologist who had previously carried out work on the Privy Garden at Hampton Court, was engaged to oversee an archaeological excavation in 2004. Also employed was David Jacques, a garden historian, who used his knowledge and expertise to select the plants for the four knots. The Atlas Fountain and aviary were replaced and Dudley's emblem, the bear and ragged staff, is prominent. The garden was opened to the public in 2009.

WARWICK CASTLE GROUNDS BY 'CAPABILITY'

The castle was in a ruinous state when James I bestowed it on Sir Fulke Greville in 1604, prior to creating him Baron Lord Brooke of Beauchamp's Court in 1621. Undaunted by the magnitude of restoring the castle, and at a great personal expense of some £20,000, Sir Fulke Greville set about converting it into the sort of fine country house that was in vogue at the time. Not only did he save the castle for future generations but he also restored the grounds, creating gardens said to be unparalleled in that part of England.

In 1750, Francis Greville, 8th Baron Brooke, engaged the services of Capability Brown to landscape the grounds, which covered some 64 acres. He was requisitioned to give the castle a more natural connection to its river, the Avon. Capability simplified the long narrow stretch of garden by sweeping it into a lawn that dropped right to the riverbank, stopped at each end by bold clumps of native trees. A sinuous drive was cut through the rock to give an impression of greater distance between the front gates and the castle entrance. Landscapes were not the only string to Capability's bow – he was also a competent architect and in 1753–55 he rebuilt the porch and stairway to the Great Hall.

Capability's expertise in creating a natural minimalistic vista at Warwick Castle was to establish him as a competent independent landscape architect and his services became sought after by members of the aristocracy throughout the country. Other projects in Warwickshire were carried out at Newnham Paddox, Packington Hall, Compton Verney, Ragley Hall and Charlecote Park. Sir Thomas Lucy engaged Capability to lay out the grounds of Charlecote Manor with particular emphasis on creating a cascade where the rivers Avon and Dene met.

THE VICTORIAN GARDEN

In the nineteenth century, plots of land located on the edge of towns were divided up rather like the allotments provided by council's today. These plots or gardens were rented to tradesmen living in the towns and they would grow vegetables, soft fruits and fruit trees, perhaps also keeping a pig and some poultry.

One such garden, Hill Close Garden in Warwick, was located on Lammas Land. This was originally arable land that became common pasture from the time crops were harvested to the following spring. Local people were allowed to graze their animals on this land over winter. However, in 1845 the land was gradually divided into plots and rented out. A well-known Warwick tradesman, Benjamin Chadband, a confectioner who lived in Swan Street, rented a plot in 1870 and bought it in 1874, erecting pigsties in nearby Bread and Meat Close. The business was to expand and became a poulterers and pork butchers. In the twentieth century Benjamin's grandson, C.D. Chadband, was still running a pork butchers shop in Swan Street which closed in 2006.

In 2006 the now derelict Hill Close Garden was identified by the district council as being suitable for the erection of fifty houses. This met with very strong objections and, due to the combined efforts of English Heritage and the Lammas Resident's Association, the plans were abandoned and it was decided to recreate the Victorian garden as an important part of Warwick's historic heritage. A variety of fruit trees, including apples, pears and plums, had been grown in the garden since 1856 but the ground had become overgrown with brambles and ivy. A programme to clear the debris and restore the trees so that they would bear fruit once again was undertaken by volunteers headed by expert Noreen Jardine.

A variety of apples are grown which include 'Beauty of Bath' 1864, 'Devonshire Quarrendon' 1676, Newton Wonder' 1870, 'Lord Derby' 1862, 'Wyken Pippin' 1703 and 'Golden Knob' 1600s. The pear trees include the well known 'Conference' and 'Commice' but also lesser-known varieties such as 'Louise Bonne de Jersey' and 'Beurre de Jongue'.

The Threatened Plants Project (TPP) has been set up to identify all known cultivars in British and Irish horticulture and Hill Close Gardens is closely involved with this endeavour. Nine plants have been recorded as threatened in cultivation and include four heliotropes.

The restored garden and summerhouses are now open to the public.

THE SECRET GARDEN

Mill Garden is one of Warwick's wonders, created by Arthur
Measures who acquired the garden in 1951. The original plot was
a quarter of its present size and, apart from the glorious views of
Caesar's Tower and ruined bridge, was in Arthur's own words, 'very
ordinary'. Although for many years it remained ordinary, Arthur
dreamt of acquiring the land between the garden and the castle, thus
opening it out to provide a superb site. He was fortunate to realise
his ambition some years later and so began the painstaking work to
render the overgrown site fit to garden.

Arthur's vision was to take advantage of the magnificent views
afforded by the castle, towers, mill, ruined bridge and sweep of river.
Cleverly, he weaved the garden around winding paths that revealed their
incredible views one by one. He designed the garden to be a haven for
birds, butterflies and insects, in which cultivated plants grew alongside
wild flowers, the whole harmonising with the cottage in which he lived.

The garden appeals to all the senses. There is the rushing sounds of the
mill race as it tumbles over the weir; swans float gracefully on the mill
pond and birdsong is sweet music to the ears; the eyes are drawn over the
painted canvasses formed by the abundance of flowers, plants and trees
(with all their wonderful textures, prickly or soft, rough or smooth);
while the nose inhales their fragrances. During the summer months there
are many-hued butterflies, bees and brilliant blue and green dragonflies
busily darting in and out of the flora. The garden not only provides a
sumptuous feast for the eyes but is a tranquil repose for the soul.

Now covering half an acre, Mill Garden is open to the public thanks
to the benevolence of Arthur Measures, who so loved it that he wanted
to share it. A small fee is charged and proceeds are donated to charity.

QUAKER GARDEN

Another 'hidden' retreat is the garden behind the Friends Meeting
House in Warwick's High Street. It was in this region that the Great
Fire of 1694 started, decimating 460 buildings in Warwick. The
Quaker establishment was destroyed in the fire but rebuilt in 1695
and extended in the eighteenth century. The garden, approached
through a little wicket gate, is mainly laid to lawn and was originally
used as the burial place for the Quakers, a tradition which began in
1660 but ceased many years ago. The garden is open to the public at
specific times and is free of charge. The Meeting House also has a cafe
serving light lunches, teas and beverages.

MEMORIAL GARDEN

The Jephson Gardens in Royal Leamington Spa were created in 1846 on land given by Edward Willes as a memorial to the famous doctor, Thomas Henry Jephson. Thomas Jephson built up the reputation of the town's mineral springs from 'a puddle of weak, briny water' first exploited in 1786. The gardens are laid out with formal flowerbeds, lawns, pond and fountains bounded by the River Leam. In the 1960s the gardens played host to the town's illuminations.

ORGANIC GARDEN

Ryton Organic Garden near Ryton-on-Dunsmore, founded by Lawrence D. Hills, opened in 1986 and is home to the UK's leading organic charity. Covering 10 acres, there are thirty different small gardens, including the Bee Garden, Rose Garden, Children's Garden, Orchard, and the Paradise Garden in which organic herbs, vegetables, fruit and roses are grown.

4

BREWERIES AND PUBLIC HOUSES

The art of brewing was originally carried out in domestic houses by women, and many such enterprises became public houses in the sixteenth century to cater for travellers. Brewing continued on premises that became known as home brew houses or malt houses and was subject to laws introduced by the Court Leet to stop the fraudulent sale of beer in quantity and its adulteration. To enforce the laws, an ale-conner was employed to sample the ale and any discrepancy found in either quantity or quality would mean a hefty fine for the publican.

Homebrew houses included:

Black Horse Inn	Shipston-on-Stour
Bulls Head	Rugby
Crystal Palace	Nuneaton
Denbigh Arms	Monks Kirby
Gold Cup	Warwick
Mother Huff Cap	Great Alne
The Boot	Lapworth
The Red Lion	Claverdon
The Red Lion	Hunningham
The White Lion	Alcester
The White Lion	Bulkington
The Wyandotte	Kenilworth

A little-known brewery was situated in Wallace Street just off the Saltisford in Warwick. This was the Warwick and Leamington Brewery Company and was established in 1832. Another brewery, the Edward Fordham Flower in Brewery Street, Stratford-upon-Avon, was established in 1831 and was to become one of the dominant breweries in the area. As this brewery expanded, the Warwick and Leamington Brewery declined and went into liquidation in 1864. Flowers went on to open a new brewery on the Birmingham Road, Stratford, in 1870 and were the first brewery to introduce coolers.

Another big brewery, H.E. Thornley Limited of Radford Semele, Leamington Spa, was established in 1899. This merged with Benjamin Kelsey Limited in 1933 and formed Thornley Kelsey Limited. Thornley's bottled ales, Sunbright Ale and Nourishing Stout, were awarded gold medals in 1920. Thornley Kelsey owned the Cavalier in Smith Street, Warwick and sold the brewery and properties in 1968, having fallen victim to the intense competition from Flowers, Ansells and Mitchells & Butlers.

Other smaller breweries, like the Alcester Brewery Company established in 1886, suffered from the keen competiveness of the big breweries like Flowers and gradually declined. Flowers had become the largest brewery company in Warwickshire by 1939 with 350 tied houses. They were taken over by Whitbread & Company of London in 1962 and the Stratford brewery closed in 1969.

The closure of big breweries in Warwickshire spawned a new breed of microbreweries. The first of these to be established was The Washford Mill Brewery in Studley in 1978 in the old mill previously used for the needles industry. It closed in 1982 having lost custom through a wild yeast infection that caused variations in the taste of beers.

Other microbreweries included Church End, established originally as a four-barrel plant at Shustoke (this moved to a ten-barrel plant at Atherstone in 2000), the Frankton Bagby Brewery in Church Lawford, Rugby, established in 1999, and the Wizard Brewery at Whichford. The Fantasy Brewery in Bond Street, Nuneaton, produces quixotically named beers such as Slurp and Burp and Woblin' Goblin.

Two new microbreweries, which were set up in Warwick in 2003, were the Slaughterhouse Brewery at Bridge Street and Walsh's in Millers Road. Beers produced by the Slaughterhouse are Swillmore Original and Swillmore Pale Ale. Walsh's Flying Top Ale won two Campaign for Real Ale awards in 2003 – at the Peterborough Beer Festival and also the Harbury Beer Festival. Also produced here is Old Gridlap.

WHAT'S IN A NAME?

The names of many public houses were associated with the crafts or industry of the towns and villages where they were located; for example, The Plough or Hat & Beaver. Some names were used to entice, such as The Cottage of Content, but the most common names throughout the country were associated with a monarch, including The Crown, The Royal Oak and The Red Lion.

The White Swan at Henley-in-Arden is reputed to be one of the oldest pubs in Warwickshire, built in 1350. It became an important coaching inn during the 1800s and from the mid-1800s to early 1900s the White Swan provided the venue for the local court and the courtyard was used for public hangings. It was reputed to be haunted by the ghost of a lady executed there. One of its more well-known landlords was Michael Elphick, who appeared in several television dramas, notably *Boon* as the character Ken Boon in the 1980s. Michael Elphick died in September 2002.

Southam was once renowned for cider making. Southam in 1754 was quoted as 'a small town much noted for the quantity of cider made there'.

The remains of an impressive cider press with a stone trough and horse-drawn wheel is an unusual find in the small village of Walcote near Great Alne.

The Four Alls at Welford-on-Avon is so called for a king who rules all; a parson who prays for all; a soldier who fights for all and a farmer who pays for all.

An unusual feature at the Blue Boar Inn, Temple Grafton, is a 35ft-deep glass-topped well in the rear bar.

At Edgehill the Castle Inn is housed in a mock crenellated castle built by architect Sanderson Miller between 1742 and 1749. The tower marks the site close to where Charles I raised his standard at the commencement of the Battle of Edgehill in 1642. The octagonal tower was converted to an inn in 1822.

The Garrick Inn is reputed to be the oldest pub in Stratford-upon-Avon. The building was occupied during the 1400s and an outbreak of the Black Death is said to have started on the site in 1564. Established as an inn since 1595, it was previously called The Reindeer. The name of Garrick was conferred on it in the 1790s to commemorate the Shakespearean actor, David Garrick.

WARWICKSHIRE'S UNUSUAL PUB NAMES PAST AND PRESENT

Arley   **Wagon of Lime**
This refers to an ancient profession where men burned limestone in kilns to produce lime for agricultural use.

Atherstone   **Hat & Beaver**
Associated with the hat trade for which Atherstone was well known.

Barford   **Joseph Arch**
Named after Joseph Arch, champion of agricultural workers, who was instrumental in forming the National Union of Agricultural Labourers in 1872.

Bedworth   **Rule & Compass**
So named to attract skilled craftsmen, notably carpenters and masons.

Bidford-on-Avon   **Pleasure Boat**
This was both named and kept by the Hendley family from the mid-nineteenth century and who were wharfingers.

Coughton   **Throckmorton Arms**
Named after the family that once occupied Coughton Court.

Dunchurch   **Gunpowder Plot**
So called because the conspirators of the Gunpowder Plot met at this inn.

Great Alne   **Mother Huff Cap**
A strong ale brewed in bygone years, which was said to make one's head swell with pride and arrogance, was called a Huff Cap.

Hatton   **The Case is Altered**
Edmund Plowden, a sixteenth-century solicitor, used the phrase during a court case he was defending to show that fresh evidence threw a different light on the proceedings. It has also been attributed to a comedy of that name written by Ben Johnson in the early 1600s.

Kenilworth   **Wyandotte Inn**
The name originates from the son of the pub owner, John Boddington, who emigrated to the United States and lived in the township of that name called after a local Indian tribe.

Nuneaton   **Rugger Tavern**
So called after the game made famous in nearby Rugby School by William Webb Ellis who picked up the ball and ran with it.

Polesworth   **Spread Eagle**
This is possibly associated with the Romans who used the eagle as their national emblem.

Preston Bagot   **Crabmill**
Crabmill refers to the way in which the mill was operated by using a horse harnessed to the machinery and walked in a tight circle, thereby turning the wheel through gears and cogwheels to power the mill.

Royal Leamington Spa   **Jet & Whittle**
Named after Sir Frank Whittle who designed the jet engine.

Southam   **Black Dog**
This name has its origins in a nickname used by Piers Gaveston in the fourteenth century for the Earl of Warwick, who he dubbed 'the black dog of Arden'. Gaveston was executed in 1312 on Blacklow Hill in Warwick and, as promised by the earl, felt the black dog's bite.

Stratford-upon-Avon   **The Slug & Lettuce**
This is said to have originated from a low-cost woodcut sign that, owing to the shortcomings of the wood carver, resembled a slug and lettuce rather than what was intended by the landlord. Over time the name stuck.

Walsgrave-on-Sowe   **Leg & Cramp**
This name resulted from a competition that called for suggestions from the public to name the pub. It was probably chosen for its humorous reference to the nearby Walsgrave Hospital.

Warwick   **Dun Cow**
This name refers to a brown cow. However, in Warwick there is a more explicit association with the hermit, Guy of Guy's Cliffe, Earl of Warwick, who famously slew the Dun Cow at Dunsmore Heath. The Dun Cow was purported to be a fearsome beast of gigantic proportions that killed and terrorised the villagers.

Warwick   **The Tilted Wig**
The name is associated with the legal profession, who carried out their duties in the nearby Warwick Crown Court in the Shire Hall. The reference may also be to the 'Rumpole' character who wore his wig askew.

WARWICKSHIRE'S WATERSIDE PUBS

Atherstone	**King's Head**
Baginton	**Old Mill**
Birdingbury	**Boat Inn**
Fenny Compton	**Wharf Inn**
Hatton	**Hatton Arms**
Hillmorton	**Old Royal Oak**
Long Itchington	**Cuttle Inn**
Long Itchington	**Two Boats Inn**
Napton	**Bridge at Napton**
Nuneaton	**Anchor**
Nuneaton	**The Crazy Horse**
Royal Leamington Spa	**Grand Union**
Royal Leamington Spa	**Lock, Dock & Barrel**
Royal Leamington Spa	**The Tiller Pin**
Royal Leamington Spa	**The Moorings**
Rugby	**Bell & Barge**
Stockton	**Blue Lias**
Warwick	**Cape of Good Hope**

WARWICK INNS THAT HAVE VANISHED SINCE 1832

Birmingham Tavern
Coopers Arms
Crowther Arms
Duke of Greville Arms
Golden Ship
Half Moon
Jolly Boat
Jolly Sailor
King William
Millers Arms
Shannon
Sailor Boy
Sailor's Return
The Bear & Baculus
The Cavalier
The Queen's Head
The Red Lion
The Woodman
Three Horse Shoes

VISITATIONS

Ettington Park Hotel, Alderminster: The hotel provided the atmospheric location for the filming of *The Haunting* in 1963. It is also allegedly haunted by the ghost of the 'Grey Lady', believed to be a former governess.

Griff Inn, Griff near Nuneaton: The inn is said to be haunted by a lady wearing Victorian dress.

The Manor House Hotel, Royal Leamington Spa: This was apparently haunted by a former housekeeper. The hotel has since been converted to apartments.

The Cavalier, Warwick: This former pub in Smith Street was haunted by the ghost of a Cavalier who, the landlord claims, was seen in the rear window overlooking the yard.

The Plough, Warmington: Reputed to be haunted by a Roundhead who died while hiding in the chimney.

The Rose & Crown, Ratley: The bar is also said to be haunted by the ghost of a Roundhead who allegedly hid in the chimney after fleeing from the Battle of Edgehill in 1642.

The Rose Inn, Nuneaton: Reputed to be haunted by the ghost of a young girl.

The White Swan Hotel, Henley-in-Arden: Reputed to be haunted by the ghost of an 18-year-old girl who died after falling down the stairs in 1845 during a quarrel with her lover.

5

TRANSPORT

A BYGONE ERA

In medieval times roads and bridges were the only means of navigating the county apart from the River Avon and the state of the roads meant that often very slow progress was made. In 1697, Celia Fiennes set out from Warwick to cover the 14 miles to Daventry 'all along part of the Vale of the Red Horse which was a very heavy way and could not reach thither'. She arrived at Shuckburgh at nightfall having travelled just 11 miles from Warwick.

In the latter half of the seventeenth century the system of turnpikes was adopted, which meant that road improvements and maintenance could be financed by collecting tolls from users. Roads that were turnpiked through Warwickshire were Dunchurch to Meriden in 1725, through Warwick and Stratford-upon-Avon in 1725 and Shipston to Stratford in 1729.

The first stagecoach between Birmingham and London was put on by Nicholas Rothwell of Warwick in 1731.

Journeys by stagecoach were at best uncomfortable and at worst, hazardous and dangerous. A fair few travellers were either killed or injured if the stagecoach overturned or, on occasion, if they were thrown from the coach because of overcrowding. It was not unknown for an obstruction to be deliberately placed on the road to cause an accident.

A fatal accident occurred in September 1782 between Coleshill and Lichfield when the Liverpool Post coach was overthrown by some timber that had been placed in the road. The coachman was killed instantly and one passenger sustained a broken arm.

Another hazard encountered by stagecoaches was the threat of being held up by highwaymen. One particular staging post at the Gaydon Inn, Gaydon, was the scene of much activity by certain highwaymen, including the Smiths from Culworth in Northamptonshire and the notorious Tom Hatton, a Warwickshire highwayman. Hatton was eventually captured at Warwick and sentenced to hang. Rather than face the hangman, Hatton cheated his fate at the gallows by carrying out the deed himself in his cell with the aid of a mat, which he possibly tore into strips to create a makeshift rope.

One evening in January 1790 the Balloon Coach from Birmingham to Coventry arrived safely at its destination outside the Bear Inn but minus its coachman and guard. These had dismounted at the Bull's Head in Meriden in order to take refreshments, at which point the horses took off of their own accord. The coachman tried to stop them and was knocked down by the first horse and then run over by the coach, incredibly sustaining little injury.

In the nineteenth century, coaching played an important role in Leamington Spa. The Royal Leamington Eclipse Post coach to London commenced running on 28 July 1828 and could complete the journey in ten hours.

By 1834 thirty-five coaches were leaving the Bath Hotel and thirty-three were leaving the Copp's Hotel daily. The Copp's Hotel was situated on the corner of High Street/Court Street.

In 1835 the fares from Leamington to London on the Tartar and Crown Prince were 21s inside and 10s outside.

In the days of coaching a familiar sight in Leamington were the sedan chairs used for local transportation. Sedan chairs were popular in spa towns like Bath and Cheltenham and as it developed as a spa, Leamington also acquired this mode of transporting the gentry who visited the baths. These were kept by Brown & Grant at Read's Baths, High Street and charges were made of 2s from Copp's Hotel to the Assembly Rooms and 1s 6d to the Pump Rooms, and 2s from the Bedford Hotel to the theatre.

CANALS

The first canals to be built in Warwickshire were the Coventry Canal and the Birmingham Canal engineered by James Brindley.

The canal system was established in Warwickshire in the mid-eighteenth century mainly for the transportation of coal from the coalfields in the north of the county and also to carry heavy and bulk goods. Many Acts of Parliament were passed before the courses of the Warwick and Stratford-upon-Avon canals were finalised.

In 1793 enabling Acts were granted for the Warwick & Birmingham Canal from the Birmingham & Fazeley Canal at Digbeth to Warwick

and also for the Stratford-upon-Avon Canal from the Worcester & Birmingham Canal at King's Norton to the town of Stratford-upon-Avon.

The new Grand Junction Canal was opened in 1800 from Braunston to Brentford and was completed in 1805, thus Warwick now found itself established on major new waterways from the industrial Midlands to London. All did not go smoothly, however, as discrepancies arose over tolls to be paid at certain locks.

The construction of the canal gave rise to considerable development in Warwick with the building of a worsted mill in the Saltisford by Parkes, Brookhouse and Crompton in 1796. These employed about 500 workers. They were able to use the canal for carrying cheap coal to power the Boulton & Watt steam engine that drove the machinery. Later the establishment of the Saltisford Gas Works in 1822 saw an expansion in the demand for coal and by 1885 the Warwick Gas Light Company had its own wharf in the basin.

The Coventry Canal, extending for nearly 40 miles, was opened in 1790 to join the Oxford Canal at Hawkesbury with the Trent & Mersey Canal and link it with the capital and the North.

The mid-nineteenth century saw the introduction of competition in the form of railways with the Great Western Railway, so the Grand Junction Company looked to amalgamations with other companies to improve their position. This led to the Warwick canals becoming part of the Grand Union Canal with the Grand Junction and Regent's canals in 1929.

The Stratford-upon-Avon Canal suffered a threatened closure in 1958 when Warwickshire County Council stated their intention to apply for the abandonment of the southern section so a new bridge could be built at Wilmcote. This was prevented thanks to the combined efforts of the Inland Waterways Association, the National Trust and the Stratford-upon-Avon Canal Society. The southern section was restored and reopened in 1964.

FEATS OF ENGINEERING

A major feat of engineering to enable Warwick & Birmingham Canal to descend the Avon Valley was the construction of a flight of twenty-one wide locks at Hatton, alongside the original narrow locks. These were opened in 1934.

Another significant engineering feat is the Edstone Aqueduct near Bearley, which features an iron trough nearly 146.304m long, supported on thirteen tapering brick piers which are 6.096m high.

It was necessary to cut through rock, creating a tunnel at Shrewley measuring 395.9m to allow the canal to pass through a ridge of high land. A rope was fixed to the tunnel wall to enable the boatmen to haul themselves along.

Although initially the coming of the railways complemented the transportation of goods by canal and was used in conjunction with them, this gradually ceased and the railway became the major system of transportation, being quicker. The canals declined as a system of transportation but their use later revived as people took to boats for leisure.

The Stratford and Moreton Railway Act was passed in 1821 and a 16-mile line was opened in 1826 between the canal basin at Bancroft, Stratford-upon-Avon, across the county to Moreton-in-Marsh, with a branch line to Shipston-on-Stour. A feature of the southern section of the Stratford-upon-Avon Canal is the distinctive split bridge that enabled the rope from horse-drawn boats to pass through the gap in the centre.

GREAT WESTERN RAILWAY – THE SHAKESPEARE LINE

The GWR opened in 1852 and the line ran from Birmingham, south-east towards Oxford and then to London. Shortly after this, another line was opened to Stratford-upon-Avon and in 1908 a third line was established which linked Stratford with Birmingham. This was the Birmingham and North Warwickshire Railway. The GWR now became the preferred mode of transferring heavy and bulk goods, which led to a decline in the use of canals as a method of transportation. One of the big users of the canal for carrying Lias clay and later their 'Cock' brand of Portland cement was Nelson & Company who had their own wharf at Stockton. These transferred to using the GWR as did many other companies.

The GWR not only carried freight but passengers also as the late eighteenth century saw a more affluent society able to travel. Stratford-upon-Avon and Leamington Spa benefitted from the increased tourism that the railway brought.

The GWR was to experience similar problems with tolls as the Grand Junction Canal had earlier. To enable the North Warwickshire line to become independent from the Midland Railway, GWR linked it up with Birmingham and the North with Bristol and the West. This was challenged by the Midland Railway who wanted GWR to pay a toll for the use of the spur at Yate, Bristol, from its main line and use its line through Mangotsfield into Bristol. The problem was resolved by the courts, which sided with GWR.

Holiday travel after the Second World War took great advantage of the railways and this era was the heyday of the North Warwickshire Line, known as the Shakespeare Line. This was short-lived, however, as motorways and cheap package holidays soon led to its decline. The demise of the section north and south of Honeybourne was brought about in 1976 by the derailment of one of the freight trains diverted on to the line.

The Birmingham & Derby railway was built through Kingsbury in 1839. Up until then Kingsbury had been a small hamlet, the main landowner being the prime minister, Sir Robert Peel, however, the building of the railway enabled Kingsbury to expand with the establishment of the coal mining and gravel extraction industries.

RAILWAY DISASTERS

A catastrophic disaster occurred on 11 June 1861 when the Wootton rail bridge, spanning the road between Leek Wootton and Hill Wootton, collapsed under the weight of a passing goods train on its way to Victoria Colliery. The 30-ton locomotive plummeted through the deck of the bridge on to the road below, killing the driver, George Rowley, and fireman, John Wade, instantly. Many of the empty wagons were piled up as high as the telegraph pole.

The accident was investigated by Henry Whatley Tyler of the Railway Inspectorate on behalf of the Board of Trade. His report stated that the cause was related to five iron girders that supported the base of the wooden bridge, which had all fractured near their centres. In particular there was one that had previously been mended and he thought the failure had started there. The method used to fix it had actually weakened it rather than strengthening it. It was thought likely that cracks in the girders had expanded to a critical size during the initial passage of the loaded train carrying coal, which gave way when the empty train returned.

On 6 June 1975 a train crashed just south of Nuneaton railway station, killing six people and with thirty-eight injured. Travelling on the West Coast main line from London Euston to Glasgow, the Class 86 electric sleeper locomotive was derailed when it entered a temporary speed restriction of 20mph at an estimated speed of 70mph. The driver, J. McKay, was charged with manslaughter but found not guilty.

An inquiry found that the gas equipment, which powered the lights on the advance warning board, was not being properly used and the lights had gone out.

LOST RAILWAY STATIONS

Many of the stations fell to the Beeching Axe in the 1960s.

Kenilworth station was closed in 1965 and, although it lost its rail link, it did not lose the track. Proposals have been made to reintroduce the station and a recent funding bid has been successful.

Alcester	Closed 1963
Arley & Fillongley	Closed 7 November 1960
Binton	Closed 23 May 1949
Bidford-on-Avon	Closed 23 May 1949
Chilvers Coton	Closed 18 January 1965
Coleshill	Closed 1968
Dunchurch	Closed 15 June 1959
Ettington	Closed 1963
Feny Compton	Closed 1964
Flecknoe	Closed 3 November 1952
Harbury	Closed 1964
Kineton	Closed 1965
Leamington Spa (Milverton)	Closed 1964
Long Marston	Closed 1970
Southam & Long Itchington	Closed 15 September 1958

Atherstone station, built in 1847, came under threat of demolition in the 1980s. The Railway and Steam Traction Society fought to give it listed status and the building celebrated its 150th anniversary in 1997. The building work won a special Ian Allen conservation award.

During the 1960s many branch lines were also axed by Beeching, including:

Honeybourne to Stratford   1969
Leamington Spa to Nuneaton   1965
Rugby to Leicester   1962
Rugby to Nottingham   1969
Rugby to Peterborough   1966

ART DECO STATION

Leamington Spa station was opened in 1852 by the Great Western Railway and was rebuilt in 1937–39 in art deco style. It is one of only a few art deco stations in the United Kingdom. The station's booking hall was refurbished in 2008 to resemble the original art deco style. Leamington Spa station has four platforms, from which trains travel northbound and southbound.

TRAMWAYS

The Leamington & Warwick Tramway was finally opened on 21 November 1881 following much debate. The idea had first been broached in 1872 and was the subject of a great deal of controversy and wrangling by local bodies such as the Milverton Urban Board, which controlled the area between Warwick and Leamington. Leamington Town Council also opposed the proposed line down the Parade. Eventually all were persuaded to get on board and a single line was constructed which ran from the High Street in Warwick to a terminus in Avenue Road, Leamington Spa, at a cost of £14,300. The line was the smallest in the country, being a little over 3 miles in length, but mirrored practically the whole history of the tramway in Britain. Horses were stabled at Coten End, Warwick and walked this route until 1905 when they were overtaken by electric trams, which ran until 1930.

The tramway crossed the Grand Union Canal in Warwick and passed Milverton station where it was bridged by the London & North Western Railway line from Coventry to Leamington Spa. Several loops were laid, including one at Eastgate, Warwick.

Eastgate was the scene of a dramatic accident in 1916 when the tram left the rail and careered into the nearby Castle Arms. The driver, Walter Mumford, had temporarily left the tram for some minutes. The bell rang, which was the signal for the clippie to release the handbrake, but on this occasion the floor-mounted bell push had been trodden on by a passenger alighting and the clippie, under the impression that Walter had rejoined the tram, let off the handbrake with catastrophic consequences. The tram gathered speed down Jury Street, hurtled off the rail and smashed into the public house, demolishing the wall and counter. The three passengers were injured but fortunately not fatally, however, the tram was irreparably damaged and scrapped. By this time the tramcars were electrified rather than horse-drawn.

The British Electric Traction Co. Ltd (BET), founded in 1895, registered its interest in the Leamington line for acquisition and conversion. In June 1899, James Lycett of the BET was elected to the Board of the LWTO company in an advisory capacity and in 1902 the LWTO became the Leamington & Warwick Electrical Co. Ltd. Negotiations with the Leamington Town Council were proving difficult and long winded as discussions continued over the proposed single track rather than a double line which had been originally agreed. The Leamington Town Council eventually agreed to the single track and the electric trams came into service on 12 July 1905.

The tram system established in Coventry in 1884 was operated by steam trams. These ran to Stoke, Earlsdon and Bell Green through to Bedworth. Trams stopped running in Coventry following the Blitz in 1940.

MOTOR BUSES

The tram system was replaced by 'Midland Red' motor buses, which had its origins in the British Electric Traction Company who acquired the assets of the Birmingham General Omnibus Company (BMOC) in 1899. The new buses ordered in 1900 were painted red. At first, operating in Birmingham as horse-drawn buses under the Birmingham & Midland Omnibus Company, the introduction of Tilling-Stevens petrol electric buses in 1912 saw a reduction in the use of horse buses and the motor buses acquired the name of 'Midland Red'.

The BMOC expanded outside Birmingham during the First World War by taking over the British Electric Traction Company's operations and opened depots in Coventry, Nuneaton and Leamington Spa as well as elsewhere.

Midland Red began operating express coach services in 1921 with routes to Weston-super-Mare and Llandudno. In 1969 the company became a subsidiary of the National Bus Company (NBC) and the deep red livery was changed to the NBC corporate poppy red.

Privatisation of the NBC led to Midland Red being split into six new companies in 1981 and Midland Red South, covering Warwickshire and north Oxfordshire, was sold on 10 December 1987 to Western Travel Limited.

Western Travel was sold to Stagecoach in 1993 and rebranded as Stagecoach Midland Red (SMR). However, on national rebranding in 2000 the SMR became Stagecoach in Warwickshire and operates depots in Royal Leamington Spa, Nuneaton, Rugby and Stratford-upon-Avon.

6

BATTLES AND WAR

THE MAGNIFICENT SEVEN

In a corner of the Jephson Gardens in Royal Leamington Spa is a very special sculpture. It takes the form of a fountain to symbolise life and is shaped like a parachute, set upon seven pillars meeting in the centre. This represents the 'Magnificent Seven'. The sculpture is both a memorial to the Czech people of Lidice and a tribute to the bravery and sacrifice of seven of their number from Leamington Spa.

The story of Operation Anthropoid begins with soldiers of the Czech army who managed to escape Hitler's tyranny in their homeland, eventually finding their way to Britain and being stationed in Leamington Spa in September 1940. Here a secret plot was hatched by the Czech president, Eduard Benes, and code named Operation Anthropoid. Benes himself was in exile in London but was determined to seek redress for the Czech citizens in Prague. The target was Reinhard Heydrich, head of the German SS and highly regarded by Hitler. He had been made Protector of Bolivia and Moravia and established his headquarters in Prague where he unleashed a reign of terror.

Enlisted for the operation were seven men, two in particular who were to carry out the assassination of Heydrich. These were Jan Kubis and Josef Gabiek. The plan received the necessary sanction and sections of the British Secret Service undertook to train the seven men who were to be flown and parachute dropped near Prague.

On 27 May 1942, Heydrich travelled to Prague airport in his chauffer-driven open-topped vehicle, unaware that a booby trap was awaiting him. His two assassins nervously awaited the arrival of the car at a hairpin bend, a corner at Holesovice that afforded the only opportunity during which the car would slow down. Usually very punctilious, on this occasion Heydrich was running ten minutes late – a fact that nearly upset the meticulously laid plan of the assassins as a bus was due to pass very soon and they didn't want any witnesses. As the car slowed down, Gabiek sprang out from his hiding place and pointed his sten gun at Heydrich and fired. It jammed. Heydrich ordered the chauffer to turn the car around and stepped out, menacing Gabiek with his pistol. Kubis came to the rescue, hurling a hand grenade at Heydrich, which missed its target and exploded near the car wheel.

Heydrich fell injured. Splinters of steel from the car had embedded in his back and his chauffer whisked him to hospital where he later died from injuries that had led to blood poisoning. His assassins, meanwhile, made good their escape and later regrouped with the other five. They were all given sanctuary in the church of St Cyril and St Methodious in Prague, which was soon surrounded by Nazis. They took refuge in the crypt and, as their opponents tried to extract them alive, it became clear that their situation was hopeless. Rather than being taken alive by the Nazis they used the remaining bullets in their guns to shoot themselves.

Outraged by the killing of his henchman, Hitler carried out brutal reprisals that saw all the adult males of the village of Lidice slaughtered and women and children sent to concentration camps where many of them died. By September 1942 more than 3,000 Czechs had been murdered to avenge the killing of Reinhard Heydrich.

THE ENGLISH CIVIL WAR

Battle of Edgehill

The Battle of Edgehill took place on Sunday, 23 October 1642 about 3 p.m. and was the first major action of the English Civil War. King Charles I took up his position at the top of the hill, on the site now marked by the Castle Inn, to survey the battlefield, an open area of fields between Radway and Kineton. From his position below the hill but under cover of hedgerows surrounding the fields, the Parliamentarian Earl of Essex waited with his troops. His task was to stop the Royalists from reaching London.

The Royalist army, consisting of 3,000 cavalry, 11,000 infantry and just under 1,000 dragoons, had the advantage of the high ground but, under Prince Rupert's command, charged downhill to engage the Parliamentarians in an attack before the Earl of Essex had chance to assemble his whole army. The Earl of Essex, considering his position to be strong with the cover of the hedgerows, held back, partly perhaps due to the formidable nature of Prince Rupert's cavalry, which had been demonstrated already in a clash at Powick Bridge where the Parliamentarians were routed. However, this strategy turned out to be a mistake as Essex could have pressed home his advantage by attacking the Royalists at their most vulnerable, while they were on the slope. Most of the Parliamentarian cavalry were deployed on the left wing under the command of Sir James Ramsay, interspersed with 400 musketeers to provide firepower, and 300 were deployed in the hedgerows. A further 700 dragoons lined the hedgerows, the infantry being deployed in the Dutch formation of phalanxes, eight rows deep.

The inexperienced rabble who made up the Parliamentarian army were unable to halt the charge made by Prince Rupert and, when one of Ramsay's troops of horses changed sides to support the king, they turned and fled. Later Oliver Cromwell was to write disparagingly to John Hampden, 'Your troopers are most of them old decayed serving men and tapsters and their troopers are gentlemen's sons, younger sons and persons of quality.'

Essex was able to maintain a limited advantage in the small numbers of cavalry still at his disposal, which enabled him to mount a flank attack on the Royalist infantry while they were fully engaged. This saw two of the Royalist regiments broken by the combined cavalry and infantry assault. The king, meanwhile, had left himself without a reserve and, after making sure his two sons had been escorted out of danger, rode into the melee to muster his troops, believing he was unassailable with God on his side. During this engagement the Earl of Lindsey and Sir Edmund Verney, the king's standard-bearer, were killed and the Royal Standard was captured by Ensign Arthur Young.

The battle ended in a bloody draw with about 3,000 killed and 1,500 injured (estimates vary). The bodies were strewn along the road from Radway to Little Kineton, which was to become known as 'Red Row'.

The battlefield is now in the ownership of the Ministry of Defence and is inaccessible.

Following the battle much plundering by both Royalists and Parliamentarians took place and other skirmishes were encountered in a bid to establish control of towns. The old Market Hall in Stratford-upon-Avon was partially wrecked by an explosion in February 1643 when the Royalist-occupied town was attacked by Lord Brooke's Parliamentarian forces. The Royalists were overwhelmed but, before they fled the town, they laid a trap to blow up their enemies. As Lord Brooke's henchmen gathered in the Market Hall to debate what their next steps should be they were given warning that the Royalists had regrouped and were advancing. This turned out to be a false alarm but, as they ran out of the building to take up arms, they narrowly missed the explosion that blew up the Market Hall.

Warwick Castle Besieged

At the outset of the Civil War, the custodian of the castle, Parliamentarian Robert Lord Brooke, made preparations to strengthen the defences of the castle between January and May 1642 in anticipation of attack. In October 1642 a Royalist army under the command of the Earl of Northampton besieged the castle, demanding that its occupants surrender. Sir Edward Peyto of Chesterton, who commanded the garrison in the absence of Lord Brooke, stoutly refused. Outraged, Northampton marched to the nearby Collegiate church of St Mary. He carried out an assault on the castle by means of hauling a cannon to the top of the church tower and firing shots. These made little impression on the castle, falling mostly into the town and killing several people.

A tract from a letter written by a gentleman in Warwick to a friend in London reads:

> There came letters to the Houses, informing the true state of things at Warwick Castle; that Sir Edward Peyto very valiantly keeps the same, notwithstanding the often attempts against him by the Earle of Northampton and his Company, who have possessed themselves of Warwicke Towne and do daily commit great spoile and outrage against any that seem well affected to Parliament.

Meanwhile the Earl of Essex, who had been otherwise engaged at the Battle of Edgehill a few miles to the south-east, was marching towards the castle. The battle had ended in a draw and, unable to penetrate the king's defences, Essex had withdrawn. Upon hearing that the Parliamentarian army were approaching, Northampton was forced to abandon his plans to compel the occupants of the castle to surrender and withdrew.

Stalwart Parliamentarian Robert Lord Brooke was later killed in the siege at Lichfield in March 1643. He was shot in the forehead by a Royalist sniper as he stood in Dam Street in front of the house now called Brooke House. John Dyott fired the fatal shot from the central spire of Lichfield Cathedral.

The fourteenth-century church of St Peter in Barford is said to carry the scars left by cannon balls. It is claimed that these were fired at the church by the Parliamentarians on their way to battle at Edgehill in response to the local landowner raising the Royal Standard in defiance.

Assault on St Mary's Church

In June 1643, soldiers under the command of Parliamentarian Colonel William Purefoy entered the church of St Mary's in Warwick and vandalised it, including the beautiful chantry Beauchamp Chapel, built for Richard Beauchamp, Earl of Warwick, who died at Rouen in 1439. Windows were smashed and monuments defaced. Not content with these ruinous acts, they went on to destroy the medieval Market Cross that had stood at the north end of the Market Place. This was done in accordance with the Puritan tenets, which frowned on symbols of idolatry.

Purefoy, from Caldecote Hall near Nuneaton, was Governor of Coventry and also MP for Warwick in 1640. He would be amongst the signatories of the death warrant for Charles I in 1649.

FIRST WORLD WAR

Some Facts About Montgomery

'Monty' was born in Kennington, London, in 1887, fourth of nine children. His parents were the Reverend Henry Montgomery and his wife Maud (née Farrar).

He was educated at The King's School in Canterbury, St Paul's School in London and the Royal Military College in Sandhust.

Not always the stalwart disciplinarian, Montgomery was nearly expelled from Sandhurst for violent affray.

Graduating from Sandhurst in 1908, Bernard Montgomery was commissioned as a second lieutenant and assigned to the Royal Warwickshire Regiment based at Budbrooke, Warwick. At the outbreak of the First World War he was deployed to France with the British Expeditionary Force.

Montgomery saw action during the retreat from Mons and was wounded during a counter-attack near Meteran in 1914. Awarded the Distinguished Service Order (DSO), he was appointed as a brigade major and spent the remainder of the war in various postings.

First World War Heroes

Cecil Leonard Knox was awarded the Victoria Cross for outstanding bravery in the First World War and further commemorated with an engraved paving stone laid in Nuneaton. As a second lieutenant with the Royal Engineers, he risked his life on the French front line.

In 1940, Cecil Knox commanded the Nuneaton Company of the Home Guard and was later awarded the Freedom of the Borough of Nuneaton. He died in 1943 as a result of a motorbike accident.

Anderson Drive in Whitnash near Royal Leamington Spa was named to commemorate the bravery of Jean Anderson, a second lieutenant in the United States Air Force. As Jean was flying a Liberator Bomber from Chipping Norton to Germany on 26 April 1945, he experienced difficulties with the plane's engines as he was flying towards Whitnash near Leamington Spa. Instructing his crew to bail out over the countryside, Jean heroically stayed at the controls to steer it away from the village and so avert a catastrophe. He was killed as the plane crashed in fields.

Leamingtonian Henry Tandey had a distinguished military career as a soldier in the Great War. As a 27-year-old private with the 5th Battalion, Duke of Wellington's (West Riding) Regiment, he was awarded the Victoria Cross for action at Macoing near Cambrai in France on 28 September 1918. Legend recalls that it was at Macoing that Tandey came across the injured Adolf Hitler whose

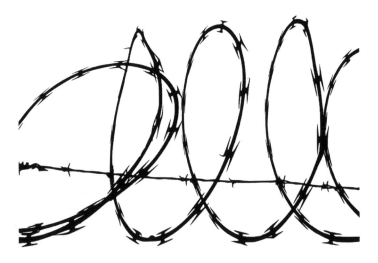

life he spared. As a casualty, Hitler was later transferred back to his own lines. Henry Tandey was said to be the most highly decorated private of the Great War, his other medals being the Distinguished Conduct Medal and Military Medal. Henry Tandey Court, off the Rugby Road in Royal Leamington Spa, was named to commemorate the hero.

Birmingham-born William Amey (1881–1940) joined the 1/8th Battalion of the Royal Warwickshire Regiment during the First World War and became a lance corporal. He won the Victoria Cross for bravery on 4 November 1918 during the attack on Landrecies, France. His gallantry made the capture of Faubourg Sayer possible by enabling the battalion to reach their objective of the lock on the canal. After he was demobilised, William took up residence in Leamington Spa until his death.

Centenary Celebrations for the First World War

Towns and villages across Warwickshire held many events to commemorate the centenary of the First World War, which began on 4 August 1914. Thousands turned out to cheer the 2nd Battalion of the Royal Regiment of Fusiliers as they paraded through Warwick town centre upon being awarded the Freedom of the County by Warwickshire County Council. The troops, which included a colour party, corps of drums and band, were attended by the Duke of Kent in his role as colonel-in-chief of the regiment.

Coventry commemorations took the form of a two-day event on 3 and 4 August, featuring specially created artistic pieces, history talks and services. Imagineer Productions staged '1,000 Wishes' in the ruins of Coventry Cathedral, which culminated with 1,000 origami peace cranes specially created by many communities in Coventry.

SECOND WORLD WAR

Operation Moonlight Sonata

On 14 November 1940, Coventry was blanket bombed in an attack by over 400 German bombers. It was known as 'Operation Moonlight Sonata' because it was carried out on a clear moonlit night. Coventry was poorly defended with only forty anti-aircraft guns and approximately fifty barrage balloons.

The bombing lasted thirteen hours during which 500 tons of high-explosive bombs were dropped with 30,000 incendiaries.

With 75 per cent of all city buildings destroyed, 33 per cent of all factories and 50 per cent of all homes, central Coventry was practically razed to the ground.

The Coventry and Warwickshire Hospital on Stoney Stanton Road, providing for 450 in-patients by 1939, was hit in an air raid in April 1941. It was reported that the hospital had been mistaken for a factory and was destroyed by a series of high explosives. A number of casualties were sustained, compounded by a further tragedy when a delayed action bomb exploded after the 'All Clear' had been sounded, taking the lives of another twenty-one patients and members of staff.

On 20 November 1940 a total of 568 people were buried in mass graves. It is recorded that 863 people were seriously wounded during the bombing, many of whom did not recover.

According to official Home Office figures, the population of Coventry in 1940 was 238,400.

Nuneaton at War

Nuneaton was well furnished with munitions factories, which made it a target. The heaviest bombing raid was carried out on 17 May 1941.

The numbers killed were 100 and 380 houses were destroyed.

All Saints church at Chilvers Coton was badly damaged. This was later rebuilt largely by German prisoners of war. Later in the 1990s, the curate of All Saints was Justin Welby, who became Archbishop of Canterbury in 2013.

Edward Melly set up an aerodrome at Attleborough that was used by the fledgling Royal Flying Corps during the First World War. He was killed in the Nuneaton Blitz of 17 May 1941, aged 83 years.

Monty and El Alamein

As a lieutenant general, Sir Bernard Montgomery was to win acclaim for his exploits in El Alamein in North Africa. In October 1942 he won a decisive victory in which he shattered Erwin Rommel's lines, sending the German commander reeling to the east. For this he was knighted and promoted.

On 30 August 1942, Field Marshal Rommel's Panzer Army Africa carried out an attack but was stopped by the Allies at Alam el Halfa ridge and Point 102. This was the second battle of El Alamein and so far neither side had been able to claim a decisive victory. Montgomery was determined to achieve a breakthrough and destroy the Panzer Army Africa through sheer superiority of forces. After six more weeks of building up its forces, the Eighth Army, under the command of Lieutenant General Montgomery, was ready to strike. Assembled were 220,000 men and 1,100 tanks against the 115,000 men and 559 tanks of the Panzer Army Africa.

The Allied victory ended the Axis threat to Egypt, the Suez Canal and the danger of access to the Middle Eastern and Persian oil fields being gained.

Bernard Montgomery was granted the Honorary Freedom of the Borough of Warwick on 22 October 1945 and in 1946 he was elevated to the distinguished position of Viscount Montgomery of Alamein for his accomplishments.

Monty became the president of the Kandaha Ski Club between 1951 and 1959.

Sheepish

At the beginning of the Second World War an ammunition dump was established just outside Kineton and spread south-west to Radway. A little later it was to acquire a very unlikely neighbour when a practice bombing range was set up near a farm west of Radway. In those days, 3 to 5 miles was considered a near miss in bombing accuracy. A large triangular white target was constructed in the middle of a concrete circle and some distance away two well-spaced towers allowed observers to triangulate the position of the bomb and how far from the target the bomb had fallen. The practice bombs were made of either concrete or timber.

It was realised that if the farmer was evicted for safety reasons, his pastures would soon become overgrown and the bombs would be difficult to spot so, despite being perilously close to the target, the farmer and his family continued to occupy the farmhouse, grazing his sheep to keep the grass down. As there was a general shortage of manpower, the farmer's young daughter would often be in charge of shepherding the sheep. A small RAF contingent based nearby would usually warn the farmer when the aircraft were expected so they were prepared. Unfortunately the procedure didn't always go to plan – a

flock of sheep clustered together looked rather like a large white target from the air and the farmer's daughter was bombed on more than one occasion although escaping injury.

One day she arrived home at the end of the day to find a practice bomb had come through the farmhouse roof and was lying on her bed. On another occasion live incendiaries were used and set fire to the barn just yards from the house, causing all of the summer harvest to be lost.

For decades farmers continued to dig up the practice bombs from their fields, even finding them in the treetops.

The bombing run would have been parallel to Edgehill. Although one of the towers has been demolished, the other is still standing in a field.

SOME FACTS ABOUT THE ROYAL WARWICKSHIRE REGIMENT

During the Napoleonic Wars at the Heights of Echalar in August 1813, Wellington watched the Warwickshire Regiment attack against 6,000 French in rugged mountain positions. He described it as, 'the most gallant and the finest thing I have ever witnessed'.

In January 1879, the Anglo-Zulu War saw a 1,700-strong British force attacked by a substantial army of Zulu warriors numbering about 4,000. The British were overwhelmed despite their superior weapon power and only around 400 survived at a place called Isandlwana. Following the slaughter at Isandlwana, a Zulu contingent under the command of Prince Dabulamanzi crossed the Buffalo River into Natal to attack the British supply base close to the river crossing known as Rorke's Drift. A small force, consisting of B Company, 2nd Battalion, 24th (2nd Warwickshire) Regiment of Foot, commanded by Lieutenant Gonville Bromhead, was detailed to garrison the post which had been turned into a supply depot and hospital. On 22 January the hospital, defended by approximately 156 men, including thirty-nine hospital patients, was attacked by Zulu warriors whose main weapon was assegais (a type of spear). The soldiers were equipped with Martini-Henry breech-loading rifles and the post was valiantly and successfully defended with most of the patients taking up arms. When it became clear that the front of the building was being taken by Zulus, John Williams started to hack through the wall dividing the central room and a corner room in the back of the hospital as a means of escape. He dragged two patients through the hole into the corner room occupied by Private Hook and nine other patients, and continued to hack through the wall while Hook held off the Zulus. Williams then dragged the patients through the hole into the last room being defended by Privates Robert Jones and William Jones and from there the able-bodied patients were able to clamber through a window and run across the yard to the barricade. Of the eleven patients, nine survived the trip. The number of soldiers killed at Rorke's Drift was seventeen with ten wounded and 500 Zulus killed.

In the 1964 film *Zulu* starring Michael Caine, the Welsh Regiment is portrayed defending the garrison at Rorke's Drift. They sing a stirring rendition of 'Men of Harlech' to stiffen the sinews as the Zulus approach. According to renowned historian Ian Knight, this is incorrect as the force at Rorke's Drift was the Warwickshire Regiment whose regimental march in 1879 was 'The Warwickshire Lads'. The 2nd Warwickshires, based then at Brecon, changed their title to the South Wales Borderers on 1 July 1881, two years after the war had ended. Their regiment comprised of men from Scotland, England, Ireland and Wales of which, according to Knight, only 15 per cent of the total at Rorke's Drift were Welsh.

Following the battle, seven of the 24th Battalion Regiment of Foot (2nd Warwickshires) were awarded the Victoria Cross, the most to be awarded for a single battle. These were:

Lieutenant Gonville Bromhead
Corporal William Wilson Allen
Private Frederick Hitch
Private Alfred Henry Hook
Private Robert Jones
Private William Jones
Private John Williams

During the Boer War of 1899–1902, Warwick became a hive of enthusiasm and anticipation when crowds gathered to witness the departure of Reservists of the Royal Warwickshire Regiment, the active service company of the Volunteers and the Warwickshire Imperial Yeomanry from the depot at Budbrooke to start their journey to the front.

The battery of the 1/1st Warwickshire Royal Horse Artillery, first raised in 1908 with volunteer soldiers, saw the most action in late 1916–18 supporting infantry. The battery came to fruition through the auspices of Lord Brooke at Warwick Castle. As a Territorial Force their role was mostly as support to the cavalry but they became actively involved at the Battle of Arras in September and lost many soldiers at Feuchy Chapel. Corporal Norman Kinman was awarded the Military Medal for conspicuous gallantry, being the first member of the battery to gain the distinction.

William Slim's brief career with the Royal Warwickshire Regiment began on 22 August 1914 when he was commissioned as a temporary second lieutenant. He was badly wounded in Gallipoli and, on his return to England, was given a regular commission as a second lieutenant in the West India Regiment. He returned to the Royal Warwickshire in October 1916 in Mesopotamia. Having previously been given the temporary rank of captain, he was awarded the Military Cross on 7 February 1918 for action in Mesopotamia. Following a distinguished military career throughout the First and Second World Wars, he was created Viscount Slim of Yarralumla in the Capital Territory of Australia and of Bishopton in the City of Bristol in 1960.

During the First World War the Royal Warwickshire Regiment raised thirty battalions and gained eighty battle honours. The major battles of 1917 saw the battalions in action at Arras, Vimy, Passchendaele and Cambrai.

The Second Battery took part in the Third Battle of Ypres in 1917 and the forcing of the Drocourt-Quéant Line in 1918. Sergeant Major C. Bull was awarded the Military Medal and later the French Croix de Guerre for his leadership in action near Elverdinghe.

The battalions of the 6th saw action at Gallipoli and in Italy in 1917–18.

The Royal Warwickshires were awarded six Victoria Crosses during the First World War.

From 1 May 1963 they became the Royal Warwickshire Fusiliers.

The Royal Warwickshire Regiment kept live antelope mascots for around 200 years. When the Royal Warwickshire Fusiliers merged with three other fusilier regiments in 1968 to become the Royal Regiment of Fusiliers, they adopted the mascot, thereby maintaining the tradition. The last antelope, traditionally called 'Bobby', died in 2005 and his head is mounted in the Montgomery Room in St John's House, Warwick. The antelope emblem continues to be worn on the buttons of the Regiment's No.1 and No. 2 dress uniforms.

7

CRIME AND PUNISHMENT

THE LAUREL WATER POISONER

On the morning of 2 April 1781 the good townsfolk of Warwick and surrounds crowded into the streets around Warwick Gaol and the scaffold near Wallace Street. Their ghoulish mission was to witness the public execution of the laurel water poisoner, the flamboyant Captain Donellan. Donellan allegedly poisoned his brother-in-law, Sir Theodosius Boughton of Lawford Hall, near Rugby, so that he would inherit the estate through his wife.

A little before 7 a.m., the dashing 42-year-old Irishman, John Donellan, was escorted from the gaol into the waiting horse and carriage draped in black and furnished as befitted his rank. The sombre procession, followed by the eagerly anticipating crowd, made their way to the place of execution. On the scaffold, Captain Donellan prayed for some considerable time and spoke briefly to the onlookers to reiterate his innocence as the noose was placed around his neck. Then, dropping his handkerchief as a signal that he was ready, he was summarily launched into eternity.

Donellan was tried on 30 March 1781 at Warwick Assizes and convicted of the wilful murder of his brother-in-law, 21-year-old Sir Theodosius Edward Allesley Boughton, a baronet of Lawford Hall. The judge presiding was the renowned Francis Buller, not known for his patience and justice tempered with mercy. The jury, twelve men good and true, took less than ten minutes to return a verdict of guilty.

CATHOLIC MARTYRS

William Freeman (alias Mason), a priest educated at Douay College and sent on the English Mission, was taken, condemned and hung, drawn and quartered at Warwick on 13 August 1595.

On 13 July 1604 a Catholic priest and his young assistant were executed on Gallows Hill, Warwick, having spent one year in Warwick Gaol. Their crime was secretly attending Mass and refusing to attend the Protestant church ordained by Henry VIII. Robert Grissold from Rowington, a young man in his 20s, was told he would be freed if he went to church. He refused. The middle-aged John Sugar was hung, drawn and quartered and his remains were put on display at the Eastgate in Warwick. As a layman, Grissold was fortunate to be spared this grisly death and was merely hanged. His body was buried beneath the gallows.

Robert Catesby, a local man from Bushwood Hall near Lapworth, is credited with being the real leader of the Gunpowder Plot to overthrow King James I and his government in 1605. Other Warwickians involved were John Grant of 'Norbrook' House, Ambrose Rookwood of Clopton House and Sir Everard Digby who was renting Coughton Court from the Throckmortons. Their plan was to kill the Protestant king and his sons and reinstate the Catholic faith as the dominant religion by capturing Coombe Abbey where the young Princess Elizabeth was being brought up and using her as a figurehead.

The plot was foiled when Guy Fawkes was discovered with barrels of gunpowder under the Houses of Parliament. When the news reached Catesby and his band of men where they were waiting at The Old Red Lion at Dunchurch, they fled. To enable them to make their escape to Holbeche House near Wolverhampton, they stole fresh horses from stables near to Warwick Castle. This plan, however, proved to be their undoing. The captured Guy Fawkes was tortured to implement the other plotters and reveal their whereabouts, and thus the king's men were in hot pursuit, catching up with them two days later and surrounding the house. A gun battle took place and many were killed or taken prisoner. Robert Catesby was fortunate to be killed by a bullet while Sir Everard Digby, Ambrose Rookwood and John Grant suffered the awful fate of being hung, drawn and quartered on 30 January 1606.

Had the plotters fled the country rather than heading for Holbeche House it is probable that they would have evaded capture.

A BURNING ISSUE

Robert Glover lay on his sickbed in Mancetter Manor, too ill to follow his brothers, John and William, in their bid to escape arrest. Known to be Protestants, and therefore regarded as heretics in the reign of Mary Tudor, a warrant had been issued and arresting officers stormed the house. Although Robert was not the subject of the warrant, he was taken into custody when it was found that John and William had fled. Robert's Nonconformity was quickly discovered and he was condemned and burnt at the stake in Coventry in 1555. His brothers escaped execution. It is claimed that the bed from which Robert Glover was taken is in the Tower of London.

In the time of Mary Tudor (1553–58), *Foxe's Book of Martyrs* notes that there were over 300 burnings at the stake during her reign. These were known as the Marian Martyrs. One such martyr preached a sermon at Baxterley church in north Warwickshire on Christmas Day 1552 and was the well-known Bishop Hugh Latimer. Latimer, previously a chaplain to Edward VI, refused to acknowledge the Catholic faith and was burned at the stake along with Bishop Nicholas Ridley outside Balliol College, Oxford, on 16 October 1555.

Lady Dorothy Smythe of Shelford Manor near Wolford was burnt at the stake on Wolford Heath in 1555 for the murder of her husband.

KNIGHT ERRANT

Sir Thomas Malory, a brave knight who fought at Calais with Richard Beauchamp, Earl of Warwick, and was an MP for Warwickshire, had a dark side. He was involved in various acts of extortion, kidnapping, robbery and rape.

He was imprisoned in Maxstoke Castle, Warwickshire, from which he escaped by swimming the moat. On 23 August 1451 he stood trial in Nuneaton accused of cattle rustling from the Duke of Buckingham and subsequently landed in Marshalsea Prison in London from where he demanded a retrial, which never materialised.

He managed to escape yet again but finally ended up in Newgate Prison, London.

While kicking his heels in prison, he wrote eight volumes of the epic *Le Morte d'Arthur*.

Sir Thomas finally expired on 14 March 1471.

WITCHCRAFT

On 15 September 1875, elderly Ann Tennant left her home in the village of Long Compton to buy a loaf of bread. On her return journey, she had the great misfortune to run into James Heywood, a neighbour and simple man who was convinced that Ann was a witch. It was his mission to rid the village of all the witches he thought inhabited it and, without further ado, he set about Ann with the pitchfork he was carrying. On hearing screams, a nearby farmer ran to the rescue and carried her back to her daughter's house where she died that night.

Heywood was brought to trial on a charge of murder but found not guilty. Instead he was found to be insane and committed to Broadmoor Criminal Lunatic Asylum for life.

Charles Walton, an agricultural worker from Lower Quinton, was also thought to be a witch. His body was discovered on nearby Meon Hill on 14 February 1945 and he too had been attacked with a pitchfork. It was said that a cross had been carved on his chest but this was not substantiated by the post-mortem. Later an archaeologist and authority on witchcraft, Dr Margaret Murray, visited Lower Quinton to pursue her own enquiries and declared that she was '95 per cent certain that Charles Walton had been killed as a sacrifice by people who adhered to an ancient idea of the victim's blood reviving the earth'. The local police detective was unable to discover the identity of his murderer and the renowned Fabian of Scotland Yard was brought down to investigate. He also was unable to bring anyone to book and the murder remains unsolved, being presently the oldest unsolved murder on Warwickshire Constabulary's records.

BLOODSTAINED BIRDSEED

On the evening of 14 November 1974, well-known local transport cafe owner, canary breeder and exhibiter Jack Taylor was brutally murdered in his home at Stratford Road, Warwick. Jack was

discovered in his home with his little dog, Tia, by his side who had also been killed. Large quantities of birdseed had been spilled from the sacks that Jack kept for his birds and it was all caked in blood.

One of the murderers had been repairing Jack's washing machine earlier in the day. Later, when drinking in a pub, he overheard a conversation between Jack and a friend when Jack said he had a considerable amount of money stashed in the house. The planned burglary went awry, however, when Jack tried to stop the robbers and was tragically murdered as a result.

The murderers were quickly tracked to their home in Edgbaston, Birmingham, where amongst the evidence found was more blood-soaked birdseed. The two men, who had previous convictions and had spent time in prison together, came to trial at Warwick Assizes in July 1975. Here they were both convicted for murder and given life sentences.

DUNGEONS AND BRIDEWELLS

Dungeons, unlike prisons, were usually located deep within the bowels of a building. They were terrifying dark, dank and odorous places designed to extinguish all hope.

The dungeon in the courtyard of the Shire Hall in Warwick was completed in 1680 with an octagonal room at a depth of 18ft. It was about 21ft in diameter, lined in stone and brick, and had a cobbled floor and central drain around which prisoners were shackled to timbered posts with their feet pointing towards the cesspool. The chain ran through the staple in the post, through a link in each prisoner's chain and carried on up the dungeon steps, passing through an inner door and padlocked on the other side. The outer door was thirty-one steps up. When more than forty prisoners were incarcerated they had to lie down sideways as there was no room for any other position.

George Fox, founder of the Quakers, visited Warwick in 1680 and wrote: 'Fifty-nine were put together in a dark hole or dungeon, underground, where they had not room to lie down one by another.'

In W. Field's *Historical and Descriptive Account of the Town and Castle of Warwick* in 1815 there is an account of the system of employment in the Bridewell in Bridewell Lane (now Barrack Street). In those times, prisoners were meant to be usefully employed and the various articles manufactured in the prison included Scotch and Venetian carpets, woollen webs, rollers, braces, Jersey, aprons, Linsey petticoats, coloured tammies, blankets, bed rugs and horse cloths. Most of the goods were sent to London, Birmingham, Walsall, Dudley and Stamford. All prisoners who worked received 2*d* or 3*d* in every shilling out of their earnings, which were paid weekly. The amount of earnings from January 1813 to January 1814 was about £350. The number of prisoners employed during this time was between forty and fifty.

Prisoners were allowed 1.5lbs of bread per day, 100cwt of coal per day during the winter months and 0.5cwt of coal in the summer, chaff beds and two rugs each. Men were attended weekly by a

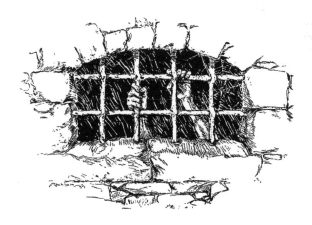

barber and inmates were issued with clean linen once a week plus soap and towels.

On the prisoner's release a donation was given according to the distance from home and their behaviour during confinement. For those imprisoned for six months, one or two shirts or shifts and a pair of shoes or jacket were issued.

A notice in *Gent Magazine*, April 1810, by Dr Lettsom stated:

> We have frequently occasion to notice the lamentable state of Bridewells and Workhouses but, as a contrast, let the attention be transferred to that of the Bridewell in Warwick where industry is encouraged and where the product of labour is appropriated to promote its exercise. It should indeed be contemplated by every Magistrate and Overseer in the kingdom.

FELO DE SE

In early English common law the term *felo de se* was applied to suicides and was considered a crime punishable by forfeiture of property to the king and shameful burial at a crossroads, typically with a stake through the heart. One such *felo de se* was Geoffrey a la Broke who hanged himself in his home in Lamintone (Leamington) in 1262.

Sir Fulke Greville, who was bequeathed Warwick Castle by James I in 1604, was brutally stabbed at his house in Holborn, London, on 1 September 1628 by his manservant, Ralph Hayward. Greville lingered on for several days before dying from his wound. The reason for the sudden outburst of violence was Hayward's discovery, when he was asked to witness the signing of Fulke Greville's will, that he would not benefit from his master's will as he thought he would. Hayward then committed suicide by turning the knife on himself, thereby escaping a fate worse than death should he be caught.

HANG IT ALL

Between 1800 and 1810, thirty-one public executions of Warwickshire residents were carried out at Warwick, four of them being female. Their crimes included forgery, uttering, sheep theft and heads/tails coining. There was also one murder, one highway robbery, two counts of rape, one of sodomy and one who had unlawfully returned from transportation.

On 1 April 1801, Hannah Palmer and her brother John were hanged at Warwick for the murder of John's wife, Mary Palmer. The murder had been suggested by their mother who died in prison while awaiting trial.

William Booth, born at Hall End Farm near Beaudesert, Henley-in-Arden, was tried and convicted for forgery at the Stafford Assizes. Sentenced to be hanged on 12 August 1812, he was put on the scaffold and, after signalling he was ready by dropping a handkerchief, the rope round his neck slipped and he was sent plummeting to the platform of the scaffold where he lay stunned for several minutes. After being revived, Booth was again placed on the scaffold and the deadly deed was carried out.

The last public execution of a Warwickshire woman was Mary Ball in 1849. Mary was convicted of the wilful murder of her husband, Thomas, and sentenced by Mr Justice Coleridge. The execution took place at Coventry County Hall in Cuckoo Lane and around 20,000 spectators were present. A death mask was made and is held in the Police Museum in Coventry.

Edward Hancock, a butcher in Priors Hardwick, was the last person to be hanged in Warwick in 1872 for the murder of his wife, Betsy.

TAKING STOCK

The practice of putting men in the stocks for drunkenness was carried out for longer in Warwick than in many other places and was finally abandoned after 1872. Moveable stocks were kept at the police station and were drawn by the offender to the interior of the Market Hall (now a museum) where they sat for six hours, watched from behind a rail by spectators who, depending on the crime, would show sympathy or hurl abuse.

Thomas Kemp, Mayor of Warwick in the early 1900s, records one amusing occasion when he observed a felon in the stocks. A small boy, urged by his mother, crept under the rail while the police warden was looking the other way and gave the fellow a bottle of water (or possibly something stronger!) which he secreted on his person. Each time the warden's attention was diverted elsewhere the fellow would take the bottle out of his jacket and have a swig, much to the amusement of the onlookers.

The pillory and stocks still remain in front of the buildings on the site of the former market arcade in Church Street, Coleshill, which was demolished in 1865. It was last used in 1863 for two felons convicted of drunkenness and is unique in Warwickshire (and possibly throughout the country) because it combined a pillory, whipping post and stocks.

William Hues and his wife Mary were sentenced for being common disturbers of the peace in June 1697. William was ordered to be whipped and Mary to wear the scold's bridle.

STONE ME

Lodovic 'Loddy' Greville, son of Sir Edward Greville of Milcote Manor, Weston-on-Avon, was pressed to death with stones in 1589 for refusing to plead to the murder of a manservant. Wicked 'Loddy' had coveted the estate of the wealthy servant, Webb, and arranged for two servants to strangle him in his bed and produce a forgery of his will in which 'Loddy' inherited the estate.

SHORT-CHANGED

As the Great Fire of Warwick in 1694 was fanned by the wind and engulfed timber-built houses down Jury Street, the order came to tear down the residence of Mr Edward Heath to prevent the fire from spreading any further. Mr Heath's house was the last in Jury Street near to the Eastgate, beyond which was the house of Dr William Johnson. It was on the orders of Dr Johnson that the house was pulled down, which was unfortunate because the fire actually stopped at Jury Street House, two or three houses before that of Mr Heath. The bitter complainant told the court it had been done without his consent and he assessed the damage to be £40. The court decreed that Dr Johnson should pay recompense of £20.

BLACK VELVET RIBBON

A downpour at Kings Newnham in the 1850s put a stop to Lord John Scott's shooting party and he retired back to the hall. When the rain stopped he noticed that the farmyard had drained quite rapidly and set about discovering why. He found a hole through which the water was funnelling and when the hole was widened it revealed a vault in which were several coffins. The coffins were opened and the bodies of Francis, Earl of Chichester, Lord Dunsmore and Sir John Anderson were found to be in perfect condition. One coffin, however, contained the body of a man who had been embalmed and was wearing a black velvet ribbon tied around his throat. On removing the ribbon it was found that the man had been beheaded and his head replaced on his body for burial. The only clue to his identity was the initials on his cuffs, T.B. It is thought that he was beheaded during the time of the Civil War.

CASE OF THE METAL TRUNK

In 1895 a couple living in Wye in Kent agreed to foster the baby son of Mrs Edwards for the sum of £1 per month. The payments were made regularly but they never set eyes on Mrs Edwards until two years later when she suddenly appeared on their doorstep demanding the return of her son. Although considerably distressed by this as the Posts had become very attached to the little boy, they handed him over to his mother. During her stay with the Posts, Mrs Edwards also acquired a metal trunk.

The boy, whose name was Rees Brandish, was the illegitimate son of Mrs Edwards, real name Elizabeth Brandish. She took him on a train along with the metal trunk and that was the last ever seen of the little boy. His decomposing body was later discovered in a vegetable patch covered with quick lime at Drybrook Farm in Ettington, home to George Brandish, brother of Elizabeth.

Elizabeth was arrested, charged with the murder of her son and brought to trial at Warwick Assizes in March 1898. She pleaded not guilty, maintaining she had given the boy to a woman on the train who was desperate for a child. With the body being decomposed and a lack of any substantial evidence, the jury were unable to reach a unanimous decision and the judge ordered a retrial at the next assize. Again the prosecution were unable to prove murder beyond a reasonable doubt and Elizabeth Brandish was acquitted.

Why had Elizabeth gone to the trouble of getting her son back only to murder him? In the intervening years she had fallen in love with a policeman from Clent, Roger Narramore, who had promised her marriage and knew nothing of her illegitimate child. Should this have come to light he would either have been forced to leave the police or the plans of marriage would have been scuppered. Rather than leave the child where he was, Elizabeth most likely decided not to risk his illegitimacy coming to light, murdered him on the train and secreted his body in the metal trunk.

'ALL RISE'

Justice did have its lighter side, as illustrated in a compilation of stories in *Memories of Warwick Crown Court* by Dee Hawke. Here are some examples of courtroom quips:

Handed a five-year sentence by Judge Harrison-Hall at the Crown Court, the shocked defendant moaned, 'I don't think I can manage that.' To which the judge drily retorted, 'Do your best.'

On another occasion the defendant, a Vietnamese boatman, had no legal representation. However, he informed the judge that he was quite content to be represented by God. The lugubrious Harrison-Hall, with his usual caustic wit, replied, 'How very inconvenient, could we not arrange for someone more local?'

8

EDUCATION, EDUCATION, EDUCATION

BLUECOAT SCHOOLS

The first 'bluecoat school' was Christ's Hospital in London founded by Edward VI in 1552 and was a charitable institution for the caring and education of poor children. Its name came from the distinctive blue uniform worn by pupils. 'Bluecoat schools' were established in other parts of the country with two being founded in Warwickshire. The Reverend William Higgs founded Birmingham Bluecoat School in 1722 and its aims were to educate the children of the poor from the age of 9 to 14 years. This was a charity school originally located at No. 5 St Philips Place and provided food, clothing and education for thirty-two boys and twenty girls at its outset. Coventry Bluecoat Church of England School was founded in 1714.

CHARITY SCHOOLS

Charity schools were significant in the education of poor children in the eighteenth century, teaching them to read and write and arithmetic. Beginning in London, they then spread out throughout most of the urban areas in England and Wales. One such school was established in St Peter's Chapel over Eastgate, Warwick and was provided for by the charity of Earl Brooke. Later Mrs Sarah Greville's Charity provided money for the schooling of poor children and in 1875 the charity became part of the King's School Foundation.

The school in St Peter's Chapel was called Bablake and boys were taught in the central room by the master and his apprentice. Girls were taught in the living room, which also doubled as a classroom, by the master's wife and his eldest daughter. Boys began their day at 6 a.m. in the summer and 7 a.m. in the winter with one hour for breakfast at 9 a.m. and two hours for lunch at 12 p.m. Their attire was very similar to that worn by the Beefeaters in London and consisted of a coat with knee breeches and stockings.

Boys at the charity school were nicknamed 'Bobdogs'.

Born in 1840, one pupil, William Tallis, went on to become a sought-after advisor to the Cadbury brothers in Birmingham.

In 1733 a Dame school was established by the Thomas Eden Foundation in Shottery, Stratford-upon-Avon. It provided education for twenty-one boys and girls aged 5–9 and they were taught spelling, reading, sewing for the girls and to recite the Catechism. The Dame was paid £9 2s per year by the Thomas Eden Charity.

The main educational influences of the nineteenth century was the 'National Society for the Education of the Poor in the principles of the Established Church' formed in 1811. By 1851 it controlled schools in thousands of places supported by voluntary contributions. In 1843 a national school was established in Alcester. Strict segregation of the sexes was practiced and a pair of two-storey buildings were constructed, one for boys and one for girls.

VICTORIAN SCHOOLS

Victorian schools were rather grim. Boys and girls were usually educated separately and learned by rote, principally studying the three 'r's – reading, writing and arithmetic. They used slates to copy on and a sharpened slate with which to write. School began at 9 a.m. and finished at 5 p.m. with a two-hour lunch break.

Punishments were administered with a cane, which could be used on the hand, bottom or back of the legs. Children who had been caned usually kept quiet about it as they could expect to be punished again if a parent found out.

No account was taken that some children had difficulty in learning and they would be made to sit in a corner for an hour or more, wearing a dunce's cap.

St John's Museum in Warwick showcases the social history of the Victorian school and children are invited to take part in learning sessions and activities, experiencing some of the discipline and hardships endured by Victorian schoolchildren.

Avonbank in Stratford-upon-Avon was one of the most exclusive Victorian schools for young ladies in 1832.

The Chilvers Coton Free School was founded in 1735 by Lady Elizabeth Newdigate and was considerably enlarged in around 1846, becoming the biggest school in the area. The rooms, with their high ceiling and wall ventilators, have changed very little since that time. This genuine Victorian school is now a heritage centre.

A ragged school was opened for forty poor children in Sheep Street, Stratford-upon-Avon, in 1832 by social reformer James Cox.

SCHOOL OF INDUSTRY

The School of Industry in Warwick, situated in Oken's House in Castle Street, was established and supported by the Countess of Warwick ('Daisy'). The objective was to provide for the education of poor girls and to form in them habits of virtuous order and industry. The school catered for about forty girls, who wore a uniform of a brown stuff gown with a straw bonnet. They were taught reading, writing and arithmetic, sewing of all kinds, knitting stockings and spinning jersey and flax.

SUNDAY SCHOOLS

Philanthropist, Anglican layman and publisher Robert Raikes promoted Sunday schools, a forerunner of the State school system. Raikes believed that, in order to stop children from the slums running wild in the streets and getting into the ways of vice, they would be better employed attending school on Sunday and benefiting from the teachings of the Bible. By 1831, Sunday schools in Great Britain were teaching 1,250,000 children weekly (about a quarter of the population). The Interdenominational Sunday School Union was founded in 1803. One of the oldest Baptist churches in the world, the Castle Hill Baptist church in Warwick (founded in the seventeenth century), introduced a Sunday school 'for the instruction of poor children' on 2 July 1799 under the direction of Mr John Mills. Although Nonconformists suffered much persecution during the English Civil War, the Warwick Baptist church was fortunate to come under the protection of Lord Brooke of nearby Warwick Castle, himself a Nonconformist, and survived. Between 1843 and 1856, when Thomas Nash was the pastor, the Sunday school had a total of forty scholars.

THE ELEVEN PLUS

The 1944 Education Act enacted a universal exam in England and Wales that allowed for a three-tier system to be introduced for 11–15 year olds. The three options were grammar schools for the more academic; secondary modern for the less academic; and technical colleges for the more vocational. Additionally there were scholarship places to be won in the independent schools. By the 1960s politicians considered this system to be unfair as not all children developed academically at the same time and many were stigmatised as failures if they didn't manage to gain a grammar school place. The Labour government introduced the comprehensive system, which saw the decline of grammar schools.

Grammar schools still exist in Warwickshire and children can still attain places at 11 years old through an entrance exam.

Bablake in Coventry, a direct grant grammar school, was initially founded as an ecclesiastical collegiate institution in 1344. It fell into disuse following Henry VIII's Dissolution of the Monasteries and was revived in 1560 by Thomas Wheatley, Mayor of Coventry, who instituted the buildings as a hospital for the boarding, teaching and clothing of poor boys. A new school was built in 1890.

An ancient tradition labels first year boys as 'fuzzers', second year boys as 'scrubbers' and prefects as 'angels'.

King Edward VI School in Stratford-upon-Avon, a grammar school and academy, is believed to be the last of the King Edward VI grammar schools. An education facility has existed on its present site since at least the early thirteenth century and it was re-founded nine days before the death of Edward VI on 6 July 1553. It is thought that William Shakespeare attended this school.

Leamington Municipal Secondary School opened in 1902 and amalgamated with the Leamington Collegiate School on 11 September 1905, developing as a grammar school under the headship of Arnold Thornton. As the school flourished, bigger premises were required and the school became Leamington College when Warwickshire County Council purchased the site of the former college in Binswood Avenue. The comprehensive system introduced in 1974 saw the decline in some grammar schools' status. Leamington College became the North Leamington School formed by the amalgamation of Leamington College and Blackdown High School.

Notable old boys:
Frank Whittle: Noted for the development of the turbojet
Norman Painting: Actor, broadcaster and writer
Brian Gilbert: Nominated to join the Antarctic Scientific Research
    Team in 1970
John Shurvinton: International U-19 rugby star

FOUR WARWICKSHIRE GRAMMAR SCHOOLS

Alcester Grammar School, Alcester
Rugby High School for Girls, Rugby
Lawrence Sheriff School for Boys, Rugby
Stratford-upon-Avon Grammar School for Girls

More recently the Conservative and Liberal Democrat coalition have encouraged secondary schools to become academies and free schools.

The Academies Act of 2010 authorised the creation of free schools and allowed all existing State schools to become academy schools. Free schools are funded by the taxpayer and are outside the control of local authorities.

FIVE WARWICKSHIRE ACADEMIES

Ash Green School, Exhall
Aylesford School, Warwick
Bilton School, Rugby
Campion School, Royal Leamington Spa
The Nuneaton Academy, Nuneaton

RUGBY SCHOOL

An historic and well-known public school is Rugby School, founded in 1567 as a provision in the will of Lawrence Sheriff. The game of rugby was first established here when a pupil, William Webb-Ellis, famously picked up the ball during a game of football and ran with it. In 1895 this was found to be a complete myth as it was established that during Webb-Ellis' time at Rugby School (1816–25) there were no rules governing football.

Its notable headmaster, Dr Thomas Arnold, was appointed in 1828 and is said to feature in *Tom Brown's Schooldays* written by Thomas Hughes in 1857. This novel exposed the bullying culture in Rugby School in the nineteenth century and followed the exploits of Tom and his nemesis, the notorious Flashman.

Dr Arnold's son, Matthew, also taught at Rugby for a time. A gifted poet, his prize poem was 'Alaric at Rome' which was printed at Rugby and his first book of poetry *The Strayed Reveller* was published in 1849.

The 'Great Rebellion' of November 1797 was led by Willoughby Cotton, a 14-year-old student. Aggrieved by the attitude of headmaster Dr Henry Ingles to the breaking of a window, the students responded by blowing his classroom door off and followed this with burning desks and books on the close. They retreated to the 'Island', a Bronze Age burial mound surrounded by a moat. Dr Ingles lost no time in summoning the local militia who read the Riot Act and, with muskets and pikes, crossed the moat and took the boys prisoners. Willoughby Cotton, along with other students, was expelled.

Former notable pupils of Rugby School included:
Anthony Horowitz: writer
Arthur Ransome: children's author
C.L. Dodgson (Lewis Carroll): author
Matthew Arnold: author and poet
Neville Chamberlain: prime minister
Robert Hardy: actor
Rupert Brooke: poet
Sir Salman Rushdie: author and essayist
Thomas Hughes: lawyer and writer
Walter Savage Landor: writer and poet

Nicholas Greenhill was appointed the first head of Rugby School in 1602 aged 21 years.

Another notable headmaster was Dr Frederick Temple who was appointed in 1857 and ordained Archbishop of Canterbury in 1896.

FOUR WARWICKSHIRE INDEPENDENT SCHOOLS

Warwick School: This school is said to date back to at least the time of Edward the Confessor (1042–66) and possibly before. It is claimed to be the oldest surviving grammar school in the world and was re-founded by Henry VIII in 1545 as the King's New School of Warwick. The school has been located in various places in the town, such as the Guildhall in Lord Leycester Hospital and later St Peter's Chapel over Eastgate. Between the late seventeenth century and 1849 the King's School, as it was then known, was located in the College of the Vicar's Choral in St Mary's churchyard just off the Butts. The building was in a poor state of repair and was demolished before a new grammar school building, designed by J. Cundall, was built on the Myton Road. The school, now known as Warwick School following a merger with the King's Middle School, relocated in 1849.

Notable old boys included:
A.G.K. Brown: Olympic gold medallist, 1936
David Byles: Guinness world record holder as ocean rower and polar explorer, Conservative MP for north Warwickshire in 2010
John Masefield: poet laureate

A tradition carried on by the Warwick town crier (or rattler) since the early 1900s is an annual visit to the school. The boys are gathered to hear the proclamation of an extra week's holiday being given, which is greeted with loud cheers.

Princethorpe College: Founded in the late 1950s as St Bede's College by the Missionaries of the Sacred Heart in Royal Leamington Spa, this school moved to its current site at Princethorpe near Rugby in 1966. The college is part of the Warwickshire Catholic Independent Schools Foundation following a merger with Crackley Hall School in 2002. Notable former pupils are England cricketer Ian Bell MBE and Jordan King the racing driver.

Kingsley School for Girls: The Leamington High School was established in 1884 and originally stood in Leamington's town centre on the Parade. It became the Kingsley School in 1949 in recognition and celebration of the contribution to Leamington made by Rose Kingsley, daughter of novelist Charles Kingsley (famous for *The Water Babies*). Rose had recognised the need for educational provision for young women in Leamington Spa and its environs, and it was due to her determination and drive (supported by public-spirited residents and dignitaries) that the school was established. The school moved to its present premises in Beauchamp Hall in 1922.

Kings High School for Girls: Established in 1879, the school occupied Landor House, the former home of the poet Walter Savage Landor in Smith Street, Warwick. It has also been located in premises immediately above the remains of the town wall adjoining Eastgate and the King's Middle School (later St Mary's Hall) in the Butts before it was demolished in 1981. A new sixth form building was erected in the Butts and opened by Dame Judi Dench in December 2006.

An unusual visitor to the school in 1926 was Professor Gaetano Salvemini, an Italian historian who fled his country when it fell under the dictatorship of Mussolini. Salvemini was an anti-fascist politician who had been arrested in 1925 for his opposition to the regime. He had been invited by headmistress Miss Victoria Doorly to give an address at the school, which was frowned upon by some officials as Salvemini was regarded as a somewhat controversial figure.

Famous old girl Gaynor Keeble is a mezzo-soprano and made her debut with the English National Opera as Katisha at the Royal Opera House Covent Garden.

The first head teacher was 22-year-old Miss Janet Fisher.

COLLEGE OF FURTHER EDUCATION

Beginning life as Thornbank Technical College in Leamington Spa, offering technical and commercial qualifications, the college became the Mid-Warwickshire College of Further Education. Following the merger of the general Further Education College and Moreton Morrell Agricultural College, the Mid-Warwickshire and Warwickshire College for Agriculture, Horticulture and Equine Studies was established in 1996.

Two smaller specialist centres operate in Royal Leamington Spa. These are the York Road Centre for art and design and Thornbank Centre for commercial and work-based training activities.

The Warwickshire College now provides 1,500 courses at different levels from basic to higher education. It offers GCSE and GCE A level academic courses as well as vocational qualifications such as GNVQs and BTEC.

The Warwickshire College, one of the largest further education colleges in the United Kingdom, won the TES Further Education national award in 2011 for 'Outstanding Practice in Sustainability'.

The Warwickshire College is an associate of the universities of Coventry and Warwick.

Two other Warwickshire colleges of further education are Stratford-upon-Avon College and North Warwickshire & Hinckley College based in Nuneaton.

9

CUSTOMS
ANCIENT AND MODERN

Rituals, customs and traditions have always played a part in the lives of communities. Some customs, often with origins going back hundreds of years, are still carried out to this day, while others have ceased and more recent customs have come into play.

An ancient custom at Coleshill stated that 'if the young men of the town can catch a hare and bring it to the parson of the parish before ten of the clock on Easter Monday, the parson must give them a calf's head and a hundred eggs for their breakfast, and a groat in money'.

THE ATHERSTONE BALL GAME

Famous for its well-televised and highly amusing (if somewhat risky) ball game, the Atherstone Ball Game is somewhat similar to running with the bulls at Pamplona in Spain. Said to have its origins in the reign of King John in the thirteenth century, the game is played every Shrove Tuesday. The tradition even continued throughout the Second World War with a head teacher's logbook stating that the school was closed for a half-day holiday on Shrove Tuesday to watch the game.

Originally started as a 'Match of Gold' played between Warwickshire and Leicestershire lads, the game is now open to comers of all ages and is played in Long Street. The rules are simple. The ball is thrown to the crowd from the window of Barclay's Bank or other building at 3.00 p.m., usually by a sporting or entertainment celebrity, and the winner is the one holding the ball at 5 p.m. The prize is the ball itself, which means a new ball has to be specially made each year.

Consternation was caused by an incident in 1970 when comedian Ken Dodd found himself performing an unexpected comedy act. The balcony constructed of scaffolding poles dropped a couple of feet, forcing him to scramble back through the window with the agility of a monkey.

A replacement ball had to be found in 1975 when the Atherstone ball was smuggled away in a car and held to ransom.

The game was threatened in 2001 with the outbreak of foot and mouth disease; however, because play was confined to Long Street it was allowed to continue at the eleventh hour.

HIRING FAIR

The 'Mop' or hiring fair has its origins in statutes from the time of Edward III. With so many people gathering at a fair, it turned into the best place for matching workers with employers and became a hiring fair. Workers looking for employment would carry the tools of their trade, shepherds held a crook or tuft of wool, cowmen wisps of straw and housemaids brooms or mops, hence the term Mop fair. Once a landowner and prospective employee had agreed terms, the landowner would make a small down payment and the employee would remove the item of his/her trade and replace it with a bright ribbon to show that they had been hired. This continued up until the Second World War in some places, although the tradition diminished after the Corn Production Act of 1917. These days the Mop operates with roundabouts and stalls only and does a round of certain towns in Britain.

WARWICK MOP

The long tradition of the 'Mop' goes back 700 years. In the days when it operated as a hiring fair, workers gathered in the Market Place hoping to secure employment while the prospective employers looked them over. They were hired for a week's trial, after which their employers could look for someone else at the following week's Runaway Mop if they didn't suit or the workers could leave if they weren't satisfied with their situation.

The Mop is held annually on the Friday closest to the 12 November (or old Michaelmas Day) and is erected in the Market Place and surrounding streets for a period of one week. Although in the past the rides and stalls once erected were allowed to stay put, more recently they have been required to be dismantled and removed between the Mop 'going round'.

Although the Mop begins on a Friday it is officially declared open by the mayor and town crier at mid-day on Saturday. The Mop Charter is read and it is customary for the mayor to take the first ride and offer free rides to some of the waiting crowd.

The roundabouts have progressed through the ages from being pedal-pushed to steam-powered and are now electrically powered through generators.

Popular Mop rides have included swing boats, dodgems, waltzer, helter skelter, carousel and not forgetting the ghost train.

Morris dancers were once a regular feature of the Stratford Mop. The dance, called the 'hay' dance, was believed to come from the French 'haie' or hedge and the morris men formed two rows that represented the hedge. They also danced in a circle, moving from the circle and winding round between partners until they returned to their original places.

MAY DAY

In bygone times a man bearing a garland of green foliage on a pole led the May Day procession to the village green. Here the pole was planted firmly in the ground and heralded the official start of festivities.

In the seventeenth century the custom of maypole dancing was frowned upon by the Puritans. The practice of May gathering at Henley-in-Arden was stopped in 1655 when the quarter sessions dealt with the 'unlawful meetings of vain and idle persons for erecting Maypoles and May Bushes'.

MAYPOLE DANCING

The custom of maypole dancing is still performed annually every June by pupils of Welford-on-Avon Primary School. The picturesque village is situated close to Stratford-upon-Avon and a magnificent maypole takes pride of place on the village green close to the village stores on the main street.

The maypole is a Grade II listed aluminium ship mast with red, blue and white spirals and rises to a height of 19.8m.

May Day celebrations in Warwick were held annually following the celebrations of 12 May 1847. On this occasion a booth measuring 70ft by 20ft was erected in the Market Square with a boarded floor for dancing and a white canvas roof in the centre of which was a maypole. The following years saw grander May Day celebrations being staged with the pavilion getting larger. In 1849 it was 140ft long and the procession included Henry VIII on horseback, Guy of Warwick in full armour and a splendid triumphal cart drawn by four horses and representing the forest of Robin Hood, with shepherds, shepherdesses, lambs, dogs and fawns.

The celebrations were not held in 1851, no doubt due to the Great Exhibition held at the Crystal Palace in London from May to October. It was practically discontinued after the May Fair of 1852.

THAI FESTIVAL

A fairly recent custom in Warwick is the Thai Festival. This started in 2005 and is held annually, usually around the third Sunday in July. A Buddist temple is erected in the Market Square and people are able to experience Thai culture through music, dancing, fashion shows, sword fighting and Thai boxing demonstrations. Other attractions include stalls selling Thai foods and giving cookery demonstrations, providing a feast for the eyes and delicious aromas.

GLOBAL GATHERING

The Global Gathering event has been held at the Long Marston Airfield, 4.8km south-west of Stratford-upon-Avon, since 2001. This is an annual music and dance festival by MAMA & Co. and takes place in the last weekend of July. The festival has grown to play host to over 100 acts on sixteen stages. It has won the award for Best United Kingdom Festival twice in the DJ Magazine awards.

ASSIZES AND QUARTER SESSIONS

The commencement of the assizes and quarter sessions at Warwick Crown Court was marked with a service at the Collegiate church of St Mary where the judges and other dignitaries would be greeted with a fanfare of buglers. A spectacle of colour and costume, the procession of Crown Court bewigged judges, clergy and the civic representatives of Warwickshire would make their way through Northgate Street to the church. The pageantry, with its origins dating back hundreds of years to when the High Sheriff of Warwickshire wielded ultimate power over law and order on behalf of the Crown, finally came to an end in 1972.

BEATING THE PARISH BOUNDS

The custom of beating the parish bounds would take place on Rogationtide in the lead up to Ascension Day and had its origins in a time when there were no maps. It was, however, important to pass on the knowledge of parish boundaries to the next generation so that matters such as liability to contribute to the repair of a church and the right to be buried in the churchyard were not disputed. All males would take part and this would involve walking around the perimeter, pausing at notable landmarks and beating them with sticks. Sometimes younger boys would also get a wallop so that they would remember the landmarks. In Whichford this activity would have taken fifteen hours, while in Hampton Lucy it would have taken half that time. This tradition had largely ceased by the end of the nineteenth century but was recently revived in Kenilworth when people were invited to join a 2-mile walk around the perimeter on Rogation Sunday, part of the original 20-mile walk.

The last recorded beating of the boundaries of St Nicholas Parish in Warwick took place on 17 May 1799. The Reverend Miller, leading his churchwardens, overseers and parishioners, took the starting point from a window in Smith Street and from there they went over the castle wall to the river where they took a boat. Making various halts they made their way round by the Leamside, Guy's Cliffe and Green Lane until they came into the priory garden. It was stated that on this occasion the weather was inclement as twice the party had been forced to take refreshments in barns due to the rain. They were also disappointed at a certain place as 'the company intended to refresh themselves but the refreshments not coming they proceeded according to the former survey'.

FLITCH TRIALS

The ancient custom of Flitch Trials dating back to the twelfth century is carried out by the Alcester Court Leet. These trials tested couples to see if they could swear to not having regretted their marriage for a year and a day. The successful couple stood to win a flitch (side) of bacon. The trials were revived in 2013 and took place in the town hall with a jury, solicitors and participating couples.

COURT LEET DAY

One of the provisions of the Magna Carta was that the Court Leet should not sit more than twice a year. At the Court Leet the steward had to certify to the monarch how many men were on his jurisdiction who were 'freemen' or 'franks', that is independent persons and not servants. Each male over 12 years could be called upon to pledge allegiance to the Crown, hence the court was called a view of 'Frank Pledge'.

King Alfred was responsible for instituting the custom of guarantees when he divided the country into districts called hundreds and every man therein had to guarantee the good conduct and honesty of his neighbour.

Under the provision of the charter of Philip and Mary in 1554, the Court Leet was vested in the bailiff and burgesses and from then on these authorities became Lords of the Leet instead of the monarch.

Henley-in-Arden maintains its ancient customs by holding a Court Leet Day. The customs were passed down through the Court Leet under the direction of the Lord of the Manor and entails checking weights, measures and quality of goods offered for sale by the tradesmen. This included bread weighing, butter weighing, fish and flesh tasting, ale tasting, brook looking and beating of manorial bounds. Traditionally ale tasting by the ale-conner involved him sitting on a sample of spilled ale on a bench in his leather breeches and if they stuck the ale was alright to drink, although this could also indicate that too much sugar had been used.

CHERRY RIPE

In the earlier years of the nineteenth century a festival was held in Warwick called a 'Cherry Wake', which was held at the time of cherry

gathering. In *A History of Warwick and its People*, Thomas Kemp has recorded that stalls laden with cherries were placed along Coton End on three successive Sundays, the dates of which had been previously notified. Cherry Street probably occupies the site of a cherry orchard, from where it takes its name.

Cherry Wakes were also held into the twentieth century at Stratford-upon-Avon, Shottery, Welford-on-Avon and Shipston-on-Stour.

BIGGEST EVENT OF THE YEAR

Wakes were originally a vigil to honour the patron saint of a particular church, which also involved secular celebrations. As time went on the secular celebrations played a more prominent part and became a feature of the wakes held at Polesworth in September until the 1920s. This was said to be the biggest event of the year and local mines and shops closed for the occasion. There were boxing booths, coconut shies, roundabouts, swings, sideshows and a fat lady. When darkness fell the whole scene would be lit with paraffin or kerosene lamps.

SHAKESPEARE'S BIRTHDAY CELEBRATIONS

William Shakespeare, composer of sonnets, poems and plays, continues to be honoured in a tradition performed each year for the past 200 years in Stratford-upon-Avon. The 'Birthday Celebrations' are a two-day event held on the weekend closest to Shakespeare's birthday on 23 April. A lively, colourful extravaganza takes place in the streets with performers, music, artists, drama and pageantry supported by the local community and ambassadors from around the world. The flags of all nations are flown from poles planted all the way down Bridge Street and celebrate the universality of Shakespeare and his works.

PORK AND FRUMENTY

Until the late nineteenth century it was customary in Warwickshire for adult children, married or single, to visit their mothers on Mothering Sunday. Mother would cook a traditional meal of pork and the children would provide delicacies such as 'frumenty'. Frumenty was a pudding made from boiled wheat grain that had been separated from the husks and plums.

WROTH SILVER

A tradition carried on annually at Bourton-on-Dunsmore is the ceremony of Wroth Silver on Knightlow Hill. Before sunrise on Martinmas Eve the parish pays its dues of 1½*d* to the Duke of Buccleuch, Lord of the Manor of Knightlow. Should the parish default with the payments His Grace may demand the forfeiture of a white bull with red nose and ears to match. The Wroth Ceremony is believed to have originated partly as an acknowledgement of the Lord of the Manor to the wastelands within the hundred and partly as a tax for the rights of way of cattle from one village to another.

GOOSE WALK

A recent custom in Newton Regis is the annual 'Goose Walk' on New Year's Day, so called because one of the founders of the walk used to take his goose with him. Walkers do the 3-mile walk accompanied by their pets.

SWAN UPPING

The ceremony of Swan Upping was designed to count the swans and mark them for their owners. This was followed by a traditional feast. The last official ceremony on the River Avon took place in around 1886.

PEACE FESTIVAL

The Peace Festival was established in 1978 and is an annual event held in June in the Pump Room Gardens, Royal Leamington Spa. Its aims are to promote peace, environmental harmony and living in co-operation with others. Entertainment for all the family attracts crowds of thousands year upon year, providing music, dance, stalls and crafts, and has become a very popular event.

WARWICK FOLK FESTIVAL

The annual Warwick Folk Festival was established in the late 1970s and attracts visitors from far and wide. This popular event provides a feast of activities and events ranging from concerts, ceilidhs and workshops to dance displays and street theatre that takes place in the grounds of Warwick School and the town centre. The year 2014 saw the celebration of the 35th anniversary of the festival and featured the acclaimed Richard Thompson, said to be 'the finest rock songwriter after Dylan and the best electric guitarist since Hendrix'.

WARWICK WORDS

The Warwick Literary Weekend began in 2002 and was initiated by the Warwick Events Group. This was the first Festival of Literature and Spoken Word to be held in Warwick and proved so successful that it continued and was to become known as Warwick Words. Over the years the festival has hosted many well-known speakers, including Beryl Bainbridge, Tony Benn, Sir John Mortimer, Ned Sherrin, Alan Sillitoe and Andrew Davies. It has celebrated the lives and works of authors and poets with a connection to Warwick, such as Tolkein and Walter Savage Landor. Events include storytelling sessions and writing workshops for adults and children.

OLD WARWICKSHIRE EXPRESSIONS

Black looks	Conveys disapproval
Blart	Cry, shout vociferously or tell tales
Canking	Talking or gossiping
Chimbly	Chimney
Coggering	Feigning illness or sleep
Ferret	Pry or search out
Gaffer	In charge, boss
Gammy	Applied to infirm or deformed limb, e.g. gammy leg
Good shut	Good riddance

Housen	Muffle or encumber
Larrup	To castigate or give a good hiding
Let's be having you	Hurry up
Like Fred Karno's circus	Very untidy
Middling	Poorly or indisposed
Mither	Bother or worry
Mooch	Loiter or skulk
Okurd	Awkward or obstinate
Quick-sticks	At once or in a trice
Rile	Fidget
Slommock	Slovenly or slouching
Spuds	Potatoes
Traipse	Leave muddy or wet footprints on the floor
Twit	Tell tales
Varment	Mischievous or obnoxious lad
Wench	Girl or female servant
What-for	Threat of punishment as in 'I'll give you what-for'

The expression 'Sent to Coventry' has its origins in the English Civil War when Royalist prisoners from Birmingham were sent to Coventry, then a walled town, for safekeeping.

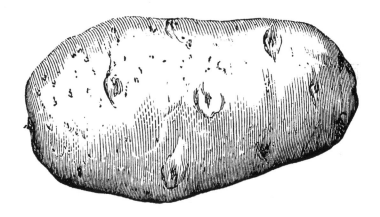

10

INDUSTRY, AGRICULTURE AND LEISURE

The streams and waterways with which Warwickshire is amply served enabled many industries to flourish. The Industrial Revolution in the mid-eighteenth century saw the establishment of cotton and fulling mills, grinding mills and waterwheel mills for steam power. The building of canals enabled the transportation of cheap coal from the coalfields in north Warwickshire to power the mills and also for the transport of bulk and heavy goods.

LOST, DECLINED, AND RESURGENT INDUSTRIES

Mad as a Hatter

The term 'mad as a hatter' is derived from the solution mercurous nitrate, which was used in the manufacture of hats and resulted in mercury poisoning. Exposure to the vapours caused symptoms such as uncontrollable muscular tremors and twitching limbs, distorted vision and confused speech and, when advanced, hallucinations and other psychotic symptoms.

A hatter was also called a planker because the hat would be formed on a wooden plank.

Before the introduction of factories, hatting was a cottage industry. The master hatters lived in the grand houses on Long Street, Atherstone. Behind the houses was a strip of land surrounded by cottages called a yard, which was occupied by the workers.

Atherstone's hatting trade was built up by brothers-in-law Charles Vero and James Everitt in the mid-nineteenth century and were well known for the production of felt hats. They were a major centre for the British hatting industry.

Vero and Everitt's largest market was the West Indies and America, where they supplied slaves with a hat called a Billycock. The Billycock was a type of bowler hat named for William Coke of Holkham who always wore one.

At its height seven firms employed 3,000 people.

Production at Vero and Everitt ceased in 1987 and the last hatting factory to close in 1999 was Wilson & Stafford.

George Nelson Dale

George Nelson Dale was established in 1837 at Rock Mills, Leamington Spa, by founder George Nelson in partnership with Thomas Bellamy Dale. The business, which mainly produced gelatine, relocated to Emscote Mills, Wharf Street, Warwick in 1842. It closed in 1969.

Animal hides for the manufacture of gelatine and isinglass were shipped from Singapore to London and then transported by canal to the mills. Water played an important part in the manufacture of gelatine.

The company turned out about four and quarter million of its popular gelatine lozenges per week as well as liquorice lozenges.

Thirty-eight steam engines were deployed varying in size from 1–30 horse power.

'Nelson's villages', consisting of twenty-three workmen's cottages and two villas for works managers, were built for the workforce and adjoined the works in Charles Street, Wharf Street and All Saint's Road.

The hall at Nelson's Workmen's Club was multi-functional and could be used for dining and as a theatre, measuring 27.4m by 10.9m and seated 400–500 persons.

In the late 1940s a gym was set up in one of the buildings in which Arthur Batty, employee and well-known Warwickian, trained Randolf Turpin, middleweight boxing champion in 1951.

Miss Mary Hooper produced a cookery book entitled *Nelson's Home Comforts* in around 1890.

Needle Industry

The needle industry began as a cottage industry in the seventeenth century with the manufacture of sewing needles and surgical needles. This specialism was introduced by Huguenot refugees who had been permitted by Elizabeth I to settle here, bringing this rare craft with them.

From 1670 needles were being made in Alcester and, by the nineteenth century, there were fifteen needle works. By 1817 Alcester had 600 needle workers. The largest industrial building was the Minerva Mill in Station Road, which was built in about 1880 for the needle-making industry and continued in that line until 1911.

The demand for needles grew and in the nineteenth century the industry expanded, becoming mechanised and factory based, employing 3,000 workers. Steam-powered mills were built to produce needles, fishing hooks and fishing tackle, and machinery and steam power improved production from the late 1820s.

In 1977 the old factory in Studley was burned down and production of 'Aero' needles was moved to a nearby site. During the twentieth century most of the needle manufacturers were taken over by the needle industries based in Studley, which became the largest needle manufacturer in the world.

William Hall's factory between Marble Alley and Alcester Road was demolished in 1980.

In the village a street called 'Crooks Lane' is reputed to be so named because crooked needles from the factory were dumped at the end of the lane.

Sterling Metals

Founded in Coventry in 1907, Sterling Metals thought it prudent to erect a foundry in Attleborough, Nuneaton, in 1939. This was through fear of competitors' action in Coventry, which proved well founded.

Nuneaton's largest employer, in its heyday Sterling Metals employed 3,000 people. The company manufactured high-quality aluminium and iron castings for the automotive, aircraft, marine and a wide variety of engineering applications. Its customers included Bristol, De Havilland, Dowty, Napier and A.V. Roe (later Avro).

Stiff competition from Spain and elsewhere led to talks of closure in 1986. Sterling International Technology moved to Colliery Lane, Bedworth, in 1993 and became Doncasters Sterling Limited.

Kench's Flour Mill

Established in 1806, Kench's Flour Mill was operated by machinery driven by a waterwheel drawing water from the nearby Napton (now Grand Union) Canal. The mill occupied over an acre at Emscote Mills, Warwick. During its 155 years of milling, the mill supplied millions of tons of flour to small bakeries, made from a mixture of Canadian and English wheat.

Its closure in 1961 was perhaps due to elimination of smaller firms in the trade and also difficulty in obtaining skilled labour.

Kench's Flour Mill employed twenty people.

The Griff Collieries

Mining had been carried out on the Arbury Estate at Griff since the 1500s and began in earnest in the early 1700s. Keen to exploit the coal on his estate, Sir Richard Newdigate made significant improvements and a Newcomen atmospheric engine was used to drain the mines.

Sir Roger Newdigate was a leading advocate of canal transport in the mid-eighteenth century and built the private canal system on the Arbury Estate which connected with the main canal network transporting goods and coal to Coventry and as far afield as Banbury. Until 1882 the pits operated under the direct control of the Newdigate family. In 1882 the collieries became a limited liability company, the Griff Colliery Company Limited, which continued until the coalfields were nationalised in January 1947.

During the 1800s the pits all carried female names: Barbara Shaft, Caroline Shaft, Clara and Marion Shafts. By 1897, Griff Clara was in full production and was the first pit in Warwickshire to raise 1,000 tons of coal per day.

A notable manager of the Griff Colliery and also a great benefactor of Nuneaton, Edward Melly came to Nuneaton in 1882, having previously trained as a coal-mining manager at the Nunnery Colliery in Sheffield.

All local pits have now been closed, the last being Griff No. 4 pit, following exhaustion of the coal reserves.

Mining Disaster

In 1882 a fire at the Baxterley pit killed thirty miners. The miners were initially trapped underground and the mine owner, William Dugdale of Merevale Hall, attempted a rescue with others. A series of explosions followed and William Dugdale also perished in the blast with his men, some of whom died later of their injuries.

Brick production went hand in hand with coal mining and in 1869 Jacob Stanley and Benjamin Broadbent took over the operation of Swan Lane Colliery and Brickyard in Nuneaton from local farmer and pub owner, Walter Handley. As the brick trade grew the need for expansion saw coal mining stopped and the mine filled in to accommodate brickyard production. Entrepreneur Reginald Stanley opened the Nuneaton Engineering Company at Tuttle Hill in 1889, which produced machines for mechanised mining and brick making. Many of the machines were of Stanley's own invention. His brick-making machine allowed one operative to turn out up to 12,000 bricks per day.

Peddle Power

In 1861 entrepreneur James Stanley established the Coventry Machinists Company. Initially manufacturing sewing machines, Stanley went on to produce the French-designed 'bone shaker' which he later developed, giving rise to the Penny Farthing. The first modern bicycle, being chain driven with two wheels of equal size, the Stanley Safety Bicycle was developed by family member John Kemp Stanley and was produced by Rover in 1885.

The cycle industry was to expand substantially in Coventry in the 1890s, becoming the largest bicycle industry in the world. In the year 1906 the Rudge-Whitworth Company produced 75,000 of the 300,000 cycles manufactured in Coventry during that year.

George Singer, together with his father-in-law, established the Singer & Company business in Coventry in 1874 making the 'Ordinary' type cycles. They became renowned for making the 'Challenge' cycles and tricycles that were aimed at the top end of the market. The company went on to manufacture small cars in 1901, producing the four-cylinder horsepower engine. The Singer 10 was launched at the 1912 Motor Show and became a best-seller. In 1904 they developed a range of conventional motorcycles that included the 346cc two-stroke.

Founded in the 1920s, Pashley, a specialist manufacturer of bicycles and tricycles for industrial and commercial use, has become a major world exporter for these types of sturdy carriers. Initially used for local deliveries of bread, milk and newspapers, their use has expanded to carry people and equipment around sites, particularly oil refineries

in the Middle East. In 1936, W.R. Pashley Limited moved to Aston, Birmingham, and began the design and manufacture of ice cream carts and station platform refreshment trolleys. The Pashley CT-20 tricycle chassis was utilised for the purpose of rickshaw-type bath chairs among others.

In response to the growing popularity of motor cars in the 1950s, Pashley manufactured the Brockhouse Indian Motor tricycles and applied Villiers engines to their own units. The most successful of the motorised tricycles was the 3cwt Light Delivery Truck. During the 1970s Pashley was contracted by Royal Mail to build delivery bicycles for them and at one point they operated the largest bicycle fleet in the western world.

A resurgence in cycling as a leisure activity has given a new momentum to the manufacture of cycles and today Pashley continues to make hand-built bicycles and tricycles at their factory in Stratford-upon-Avon.

Rev Up

Entrepreneur Harry Lawson kick-started the motor industry in Coventry when he acquired a factory from the Coventry Cotton Spinning and Weaving Company and installed his new car firms. It was called 'The Motor Mills' and the first Daimler car emerged in 1896.

The Swift Cycle Company established in 1896 evolved from the Coventry Sewing Machine Company founded by James Starley. The Swift Cycle Company progressed from making bicycles in 1869 to making motorcycles in 1898 and produced their first single-cylinder car in 1900 using an MMC engine. The last Swift car to be produced was the 1930 Cadet with an 850cc Coventry Climax engine. It was priced at £149 for the tourer and £165 for the saloon. The company closed in 1931, unable to compete with Ford and Morris.

Donald Healey founded his sports car business in 1945 in a disused aircraft components factory off Millers Road in Warwick. Together with Roger Menadue from Armstrong Whitworth, he ran an experimental workshop. Healey also opened a showroom at Coten End in Warwick. In 1948 the Elliott saloon was introduced. Reaching a top timed speed of 104.7mph over 1 mile it was claimed to be the fastest of its kind in the world. The Silverstone, a sporting car, was introduced in 1949 with a top speed of 107mph. In 1952 a joint venture with the British Motor Corporation produced the Austin-Healey Marque and later, the Austin-Healey Sprite.

Founded in 1919 by Thomas George John, T.G. John & Company Limited began life as a factory off the Holyhead Road, Coventry, producing stationary engines, carburetors and motor scooters. It became the Alvis Car & Engineering Company Limited in 1921 with its logo as The Red Triangle and a second factory was established in Holyhead Road in 1935, producing armoured vehicles. The factory was severely damaged by bombing raids on Coventry in 1940 although its capacity to produce military equipment survived. In 1923 Alvis introduced their highly successful sports car, the 12/50. Alvis became a subsidiary of Rover in 1965 when the production of cars ceased although military vehicles continued to be made.

Leon L'Hollier was prosecuted for speeding on 22 December 1895. L'Hollier was found to have travelled at speeds of up to 6mph in Shirley, contravening the 1878 Locomotives on Highways Act that stipulated a speed of not more than 4mph. Despite committing the offence in a vehicle rather than a steam-traction engine for which the Act had been devised, he was found guilty and fined 1*s* plus costs.

British Small Arms Company Limited
The British Small Arms Company (BSA) started up in 1861, purchasing 25 acres of land at Small Heath, Birmingham, where it built its factory. They produced the Martini Henry rifle in 1874, the weapon used to defend the British supply base at Rorke's Drift, and also Lewis guns. BSA was a major producer of armaments in Birmingham for 125 years but as demand declined they diversified and adapted their machinery to produce cycle parts. BSA also adapted the gun trade to produce rifles for sporting activities and target practice. They entered the motorcycle trade in 1910 and became the largest motorcycle producer in the world. The company also acquired Daimler in Coventry with BSA shares, however, this merger didn't go well and BSA continued to produce their own cars using Daimler

engines. BSA folded in 1973 and BSA Guns and other parts of the organisation were bought out by Manganese Bronze, who was then the owner of Norton Villiers.

Flavel and the Russian Vapour Bath

When Russian Count Sabloukoff visited the saline bathing facilities in Leamington Spa in 1815 he was disappointed to find that there wasn't a vapour bath, something that he was accustomed to enjoying in Russia. A Leamington entrepreneur, William Flavel, who had established his ironworks in 1803, made the Russian Vapour Bath and, with the growing popularity of bathing establishments around the newfound springs, expanded his business. He made baths that could be hired or purchased and, as the business flourished, he diversified in 1829 by patenting a new register cooking grate, the 'Kitchener'.

William Flavel established the Eagle Foundry in the 1830s to cater for the demand for the 'Kitchener'. When he died in 1844, his son Sidney took over the firm and exhibited the 'Kitchener' at the Great Exhibition, Crystal Palace in 1851. The 'Kitchener' was to become an award winner worldwide and featured in the kitchens of royalty.

The popular 'Debonair' gas fire was launched in August 1961. This was followed by the 'Equerry' automatic gas cooker in 1962.

Flavel-Leisure was the first British manufacturer to introduce cookers with a gas hob and electric oven in 1984.

Home Cooking the Flavel Way was produced in 1952, compiled by Miss Ann Cutteridge.

The business still located in Royal Leamington Spa now operates under the name of Aga Rangemaster.

Rotherham's Watchmakers

Coventry was once one of three main centres in the United Kingdom involved in watch and clock manufacturing, the others being Liverpool and London. The watch and clock makers inhabited workshops over houses in Spon Street, known as top shops and which were previously the domain of the ribbon weavers.

A major employer was the firm of Rotherham & Sons, first founded by Samuel Vale in 1747. It then became Vale & Howlette; Vale, Howlette, Carr & Rotherham; and Rotherham & Sons. By 1899 the firm employed 400–500 people, with an additional 200 outworkers, and produced 100 watches a day.

The famous Godiva Clock in Broadgate, where Lady Godiva and Peeping Tom appears on the hour, houses the clock movement made by E.T. Loseby in 1831. Loseby was an apprentice at Rotherham's and made the movement for the clock in the Market Hall. When the Market Hall was dismantled in 1942 the clock movement was saved and later transferred to its present home.

Writer of classics, Charles Dickens visited the works in 1858 and was presented with a gold watch.

The watch-making industry fell into decline in the 1930s as other industries took off, including the manufacture of motorcycles, automobiles, machine tools and aircrafts.

A blue plaque on the former buildings housing Rotherham's in Spon Street commemorates the establishment of the firm in 1750 by founder Samuel Vale.

William Glover

The 1851 census records William Glover as a wheelwright and agriculture implement manufacturer, employing four men at the Eagle Works in the Saltisford, Warwick. In 1891 Glover & Sons took over the business of wagons and cart builders and were awarded a prize by the London County Council for the best dustcart. Established in the Saltisford and the Packmores, their engineering department also produced roller mill plants, cement-making machinery and constructional ironwork for barns and churches. Glover & Sons was succeeded by the Eagle Engineering Company in 1911.

AGRICULTURE

Hedge Cutter Extraordinaire

The compact village of Barford is approached over a four-arched picturesque bridge built in 1785 and spanning the River Avon. The village, called Bereforde in Domesday Book, was an Anglo-Saxon ford 'which can carry a load of barley'. A public house on Bridge Street, The Joseph Arch, is named to commemorate Barford's famous son born in 1826.

Joseph Arch started his agricultural life as a hedge cutter, becoming the champion hedge cutter of England. Disillusioned by the poor wages and long working hours experienced by agricultural workers, Joseph Arch set up a meeting in the sixteenth-century Stag Inn in nearby Wellesbourne. The popular event attracted 500 workers and Arch urged them to press for an increase of 6d per day on their weekly wages, together with a cut in hours to nine hours per day. The result of the meeting was the creation of the Warwickshire Union of Farm Workers.

Following a number of strikes, Arch then sought to nationalise the union and in 1872 he was appointed a full-time president of the National Agricultural Labourers Union at £2 per week. Not one to rest on his laurels, Arch went on to get elected as a Liberal MP for north-west Norfolk in 1885, having the distinction of being the first farm labourer ever to enter Parliament. He died in 1919 and is buried in the local churchyard.

Jubilations

Stoneleigh Park has played host to the Royal Agricultural Show since 1968 with a final show taking place in 2009. The show featured farming, food and rural life with exhibitions of the finest

breeds of livestock, demonstrations and new businesses and technological improvements.

The first show lasted for four days and attracted 111,916 visitors.

Torrential rain forced the show to close early in July 2007 for the first time in its history, when the showground became a sea of mud.

The queen and Duke of Edinburgh visited the show on 3 July 2002 as part of the queen's Golden Jubilee tour.

Restoration, Restoration, Restoration

Chedham's Yard in Wellesbourne was originally purchased by Wellesbourne Parish Council in 2002 in a dilapidated state but was deemed to be worth conserving as a rare example of a blacksmith's forge.

It won BBC Television series *Restoration Village* in 2006 when it tipped the poll of eight finalists in the country. It was restored with prize money and Heritage Lottery funds, and is now a rare and well-preserved example of village life in a bygone era.

The nineteenth-century blacksmith and wheelwright shop closed in 1965 when owner Bill Chedham left. It was reopened on 6 June 2012 and is intended to function as a working museum with a blacksmith providing training and education. Chedham's Yard, consisting of a collection of workshops crammed with tools, equipment and items made on site, is open to the public on a pre-booked basis and visits are planned to last from 1.5–2 hours.

Agricultural Revolution

Throughout the eighteenth century, Warwickshire was subjected to 175 Enclosure Acts. Enclosures of the open-field system enabled more efficient production but had the unfortunate effect of displacing people who used the land for farming and grazing their animals or gathering timber.

The first enclosure was in Lighthorne in 1720 and the last was in Langley in 1835.

Prior to enclosures many open fields were cultivated using the four crop rotation system introduced in 1730 by 'Turnip' Townshend. This practice was being used in the open fields at Coleshill until 1780 when 900 acres were enclosed.

William Shakespeare became involved in the enclosure dispute as he had purchased a half share in a lease of tithes in Welcombe near Stratford-upon-Avon and he portrayed the social discord caused by enclosures in his plays, *King Lear* and *As You Like It*.

The agricultural revolution saw a significant improvement in livestock breeding in the eighteenth century and enclosures enabled farmers to experiment with their own animals. Agricultural innovator, the Earl of Aylesford at Packington, experimented with breeding sheep and used both Wiltshire breeds and Spanish Merinos on his farms in the early nineteenth century.

In the twenty years following the enclosures of its common fields in 1779, the population of Napton dropped from 900 to 787.

On 23 September 1835 some 200 villagers of Pailton rioted. This was in response to the Earl of Denbigh's wholesale requisition of their holdings, depriving them of their living.

A Piece of Green Cheese

The enclosures during the reign of King James I had a devastating effect, depriving the common man of his strips of land for ploughing, grazing rights and ability to gather timber. It led to widespread depopulation of the countryside, which gave rise to beggars and vagabonds wandering from parish to parish. The upshot of these enclosures was widespread rioting.

In 1607 the Midland Revolt, which attracted 1,000 rioters, started in Haselbech in Northamptonshire and quickly spread to Warwickshire and Leicestershire. It was led by John Reynolds, a tinker who was known as 'Captain Pouch' because of a pouch he always carried at his side. He urged his followers not to use violence but level or dig up the enclosures. They became known as Levellers or Diggers. Reynolds promised to keep them safe by the contents of his pouch. When he was captured the pouch was opened and found to contain nothing more than a piece of green cheese. Reynolds was hanged and, of the Levellers that were taken prisoner, some suffered the grisly fate of being hung, drawn and quartered.

By Troth
The Old Swan Foundry in Langley was founded by William Troth in 1854 and was originally powered by a waterwheel he had made himself.

Troth was known locally as the 'Iron Duke' because he built himself a cart with iron wheels and used this to advertise his business. He was most famous for the single-furrow horse-drawn composite cast-iron plough.

In the 1880s eighty ploughs were made annually but had dropped to twenty by 1939.

In spite of its small size, the foundry had a considerable influence on the local farming community. It would eventually close in 1965.

A Miscellany of Interesting Facts
Agricultural reformer Joseph Russell farmed in Cubbington near Leamington Spa from 1780–1820. He invented a revolutionary clover head-gathering machine.

The National Maize Demonstration was held in October 1975 on Clyde Higgs' farm at Snitterfield, the largest farm in Warwickshire.

In the late nineteenth century the village of Harbury was known as 'Hungry Harbury' because its soil was less fertile than in other parts of the county and more difficult to work.

Leamington Priors (now Royal Leamington Spa) was stated, at the time of Domesday in 1086, to be two hides in extent, equal to about 200 acres of land. It was then valued at £4 and two mills stood within its precincts.

The land belonging to St Mary's church in Warwick is recorded in Domesday as: 'Of Turchill the Church of St Mary in Warwick holds 1 hide in Moitone. The arable is 1 ploughland. There are 3 bordars with 1 plough and 1 bondswoman. There are 4 acres of meadow.' It was valued at 5s.

The National Vegetable Research Station at Wellesbourne was established in 1949 in response to post-war pressure for food production. It became the Warwick Horticultural Research International on 1 April 2004 and is now operated by the University of Warwick.

The practice of setting fire to stubble once crops have been harvested was banned in 1963 due to the smoke causing atmospheric pollution.

The four crop rotation system made up of a cycle of clover, roots and two cereals introduced by 'Turnip' Townshend in 1730 was adopted at Coleshill before 900 acres of the open fields were enclosed in 1780.

Southam was a stopping place on the route of Welsh drovers. In medieval times the Welsh drovers transported cattle from North Wales to the markets of the south-east of the country, their route taking them through Kenilworth, Cubbington, Offchurch, Southam and Priors Hardwick in Warwickshire. Roads in Southam called Welsh Road East and West were probably used for the purpose of droving.

LEISURE

As a half-day holiday on Saturday became more widespread, football as a leisure activity became increasingly popular. The first local match to be played between Stratford and Birmingham was in 1873.

Boating

As canals declined as a means of transporting bulky goods, particularly coal, their uses lapsed until they were later revived for pleasure boating. The restoration of the southern section of the Stratford Canal, opened in 1964, was a turning point for the waterways movement in Britain. During the 1960s pleasure boating began to grow in popularity and replaced the old trading boats. The Birmingham Fazeley Canal flowing through Curdworth was one of the first in the country to be reclaimed from industrial decay and Curdworth is now a delightful location for walks and pleasure boating.

In the mid-1970s the Upper Avon Navigation, which had been derelict for more than a century, was reopened by the Queen Mother and the canal became part of a navigable route through to the River Severn once again.

Eccentric nineteenth-century novelist Marie Corelli, author of *The Sorrow of Satan* and others, imported a gondola complete with gondolier from Venice. While living in Stratford-upon-Avon, Ms Corelli frequently used her leisure time to sail to and fro on the River Avon with her companion. Together with her friend she also regularly drove a carriage around Stratford with her two ponies, Puck and Ariel.

An exciting day out is now offered by Warwick Boats. Dragon Boat racing is available either as a team-building activity, a charity event or a great day out.

Five boat hire companies for Warwickshire:

Avon Boating	Swans Nest Boathouse, Swans Nest, Stratford-upon-Avon
Warwick Boats	St Nicholas Park, Banbury Road, Warwick
Kate Boats Warwick Ltd	Nelson Lane, Warwick

Rose Narrowboats   Fosse Way, Stretton-Under-Fosse,
                            near Rugby
Willow Wren   Warwickshire Ring Boat Hire, Rugby

Gliding

Gliding in the United Kingdom began as a leisure activity in the 1930s and has continued to grow in popularity. Stratford-upon-Avon Gliding Club was first formed at Long Marston Airfield on 4 April 1974 by ex-members of the defunct Worcestershire Gliding Club. The first flight at Long Marston was on Good Friday, 12 April 1974 in a Schleicher Ka2, a two-seat training glider, with pilots Jim Tyler and Glyn Rogers. Due to difficulties experienced at Long Marston, the club moved to the disused Snitterfield Airfield between Snitterfield and Bearley in 1987and now operate from there. The club celebrated their 40th anniversary on 4 April 2014.

Glider pilots at the Stratford Gliding Club range in age from 14 years to 80+ and come from all walks of life. The club is an accredited Junior Gliding Centre.

The club's height record is 11,800ft and was achieved by Sharon Kerby in August 2011 in a Schleicher ASK24. The longest distances flown from the club and back took place on 8 August 2007 when two members, flying in company with each other, flew virtually the same distance. The distance covered by Phil King in an LS8 glider was 751.7km in nine hours, two minutes and Martyn Davies (also flying an LS8) managed 751.2km in nine hours, twelve minutes. The significance of these flights were that they were achieved from winch launches to heights of about 1,200ft and it is believed that they are the only 750km flights ever carried out from winch launches in this country.

Tee Off

Kenilworth Golf Club, one of the oldest in Warwickshire, was founded in 1889 and located at the Castle Farm Course. This was to play an important part in expanding the growth and interest in the game in Warwickshire. The construction of the 9-hole course was supervised by golf professional Jack Burns, who won the Open Championship at St Andrews in 1888. The opening day saw Harold Hilton set a course record of 71. By 1900 the Warwickshire Ladies County Golf Association was established.

Other Warwickshire golf clubs:

Bidford Grange Golf & Country Club	Bidford-on-Avon
Bramcote Waters	Bazzard Road, Bramcote, Nuneaton
Haven Pastures	Stratford Road, Henley-in-Arden
Ingon Manor	Ingon Lane, Snitterfield, near Stratford-upon-Avon
Leamington & County	Golf Lane, Whitnash, near Royal Leamington Spa
Newbold Comyn	Newbold Terrace East, Royal Leamington Spa
Nuneaton Golf Club	Golf Drive, Whitestone, Nuneaton
Oakridge	Arley Lane, Ansley Village, Nuneaton
Purley Chase Golf & Country Club	Pipers Lane, Ridge Lane, near Nuneaton
Rugby Golf Club	Clifton Road, Rugby
Stratford Oaks	Bearley Road, Snitterfield, Stratford-upon-Avon
Warwick Golf Centre	Warwick Racecourse, Warwick
The Warwickshire	Leek Wootton, near Warwick

Horse Racing

Warwick Racecourse is one of the oldest in the country and can claim a history of racing dating back to the 1700s. In 1707 Lord Brooke gave £15 to the chamberlains 'towards making a horse race' and by 1775 the races held in September provided entertainment on two days. Racing as a leisure activity increased in popularity and a race stand was erected in 1809. The *Sporting Magazine* claims that at least 50,000 spectators attended a race meeting in 1825. In the 1890s Warwick Racecourse was home to the National Hunt Chase, which was second only to the Grand National. The social round was complemented by race balls, hunt balls, concerts, winter assemblies and card parties.

Parks

The first parks were deer parks, created in medieval times specifically for the aristocracy to hunt deer. Parkland was later developed around grand houses by landscape artists such as Capability Brown for the wealthy to stroll around. In the Victorian era especially, stemming from the Industrial Revolution, the park became a municipal open space purposely created within towns and free for the adult masses to stroll in, take the air and feel at one with nature. Urban parks were increasingly used for sporting pursuits and their popularity as places for leisure activities grew in the twentieth century.

St Nicholas Park in Warwick was once meadowland called St Nicholas Meadow. In the 1930s Warwick Borough Council purchased the site in response to the town's growth and formal gardens and children's gardens were laid out. The eastern side of the meadow was laid out as playing fields after the Second World War and an outdoor swimming pool was provided for public use. More recently the use of the park has expanded to accommodate an indoor leisure centre with a pool, children's fairground rides and a mini golf course, formal gardens and sports pitches. Situated on the banks of the River Avon, the park's leisure activities also include pleasure boating.

Other parks include:

The Jephson Gardens	Royal Leamington Spa	(Formal gardens, cafes)
Victoria Park	Royal Leamington Spa	(Tennis court and paddling pool)
Abbey Fields	Kenilworth	(Outdoor swimming pool)

11

NOTABLE PEOPLE AND SPORTS PERSONALITIES

Television presenter, radio broadcaster and celebrity chef Anthony Worrall-Thompson was born in Stratford-upon-Avon. His programmes have included *Ready, Steady, Cook* and *Saturday Kitchen* and he has won the Meilleur Ouvrier de Grande Bretagne award.

Popular television actress Felicity Kendall was born in Olton. She is best known for television series *The Good Life* and *Rosemary & Thyme*.

In 1819, novelist, journalist and translator George Eliot was born Mary Ann Evans at South Farm on the Arbury Estate. Arbury Hall features in her *Scenes of Clerical Life* as Cheverel Manor and Nuneaton as the town of 'Milby'. Her many novels included *Mill on the Floss*, *Silas Marner* and *Middlemarch*. She died in 1880 and a hospital was named after her – the George Eliot Hospital in Nuneaton.

John Wyndham (Parkes Lucas Beynon Harris, 1903–69) was born in the village of Dorridge, close to Knowle. As a science-fiction writer, his best-known work was *The Day of the Triffids* but his earlier works, which included *Foul Play* were written using the name John Beynon.

English film and television director Ken Loach was born in Nuneaton. His films include *Kes* in 1969 and *The Wind that Shakes the Barley* in 2006.

Norman George Painting, OBE (1924–2009) was born in Leamington Spa. A writer, broadcaster and actor, Norman was best known for his radio character, Phil Archer, in the long-running series *The Archers*.

He appeared in the *Guinness Book of World Records* holding the record for playing the longest continuous role (fifty-nine years). He also became the patron of Age Concern Warwickshire.

Jeremy Brett was born Peter Jeremy William Huggins in Berkswell (1933–95). He was an actor best known for playing the title role in television series *Sherlock Holmes*. His father was Lord Lieutenant of Warwickshire.

Founder of Rugby School, Lawrence Sheriff was born in Rugby (1510–67). He was purveyor of spices to Elizabeth I.

Born in Bedworth, Nick Skelton was an Olympic gold medal winner in 2012 in the men's team show jumping.

Randolf Turpin (1928–66) was born in Leamington Spa. He was Boxing Middleweight Champion in 1951 when he beat the American, Sugar Ray Robinson and went on to win the Lonsdale Belt.

A baronet and MP, Sir Roger Newdigate was born in Arbury (1719–1806). He was also an English antiquary and gave money to found the Newdigate Prize for English Verse at Oxford University.

Rupert Brooke (1887–1915) was born in Rugby. He is best known as a war poet, especially for the sonnet, 'The Soldier'. His most famous collection of poems, which included all five sonnets, was first published in 1915. He was a member of the 'Bloomsbury' Set and Virginia Woolf claimed she had been skinny-dipping with him when they were both at Cambridge. Rupert Brooke is buried on the Greek island of Skiathos.

Walter Savage Landor (1775–1864) was born in Eastgate House, Warwick, now part of the King's High School for Girls. As a young man he was headstrong and managed to get himself kicked out of Rugby School and Oxford where he was known as a 'mad Jacobin' because of his informal dress code. Walter Landor was best known for his prose *Imaginary Conversations* in which he drew on a vast array of historical characters from Greek philosophers to contemporary writers and composed conversations between pairs of characters. He wrote over 300 Latin poems, political tracts and essays.

Warwick's famous son, Thomas Oken (*c.* 1509–73), was a rich mercer dealing in textiles and silks and a great benefactor to the town.

When Henry VIII dissolved the guilds, Oken masterminded the transfer of assets from the guilds and the Church to the Corporation and other charitable funds before they could be seized by the Crown, an extremely wily and astute move. This was achieved through clever negotiations with the king's commissioners. He is credited with the establishment of the Henry VIII Charity, which today still benefits schools, organisations and residents. Oken's own charity provided for almshouses and poor people in the town.

A playwright, poet and actor, William Shakespeare (1564–1616) and his works are still universally acclaimed over 400 years later. He became a managing partner in the Lord Chamberlain's Men, an acting company in London, and by 1599 he and business partners had built their own theatre on the south bank of the Thames called the Globe. His first play is thought to be *Henry VI, Part II*, which was first performed in 1590–91. Very little is known about him between the years 1585–92 and this period has been referred to as 'Shakespeare's lost years'. Shakespeare is said to have portrayed Sir Thomas Lucy, owner of Charlecote Park, as Justice Shallow in *The Merry Wives of Windsor*. This is thought to have been in retaliation

for when Sir Thomas caught the young Shakespeare poaching deer. He married Anne Hathaway who was eight years his senior and they had three children: Susanna and twins Hamnet and Judith. Shakespeare was born in Stratford-upon-Avon.

In 1603 Robert Baron Spencer of Wormleighton was considered to be the richest man in England, having inherited both the Wormleighton and Althorp estates where the family continued to graze enormous flocks of sheep and herds of cattle.

Sir Frank Whittle (1907–96) was born in Earlsdon, Coventry and educated at Leamington College for Boys. Beginning his officer training course at RAF Cranwell, he went on to graduate from the University of Cambridge with a First and rose through the ranks to become air commodore. Noted for his development of the turbojet, the first flight of an Allied turbojet, the Gloster E28/29, was made on 15 May 1941 at RAF Cranwell. He won the Charles Stark Draper Prize, Legion of Merit award for his pioneering engineering work. Sir Frank retired from the RAF in 1948 and received a knighthood.

Larry Grayson (1923–95) was born William Sulley White in Banbury and was adopted by a family in Nuneaton where he spent most of his life. A comedian and television presenter, Grayson was best remembered for *The Generation Game* in 1978, which attracted audiences of up to 24 million per week. He also had his own show, *Shut That Door*, which became his catchphrase and in which he referred to characters Everard, Apricot Lil and Slack Alice. His last public appearance was on 3 December 1994 at the 'Royal Variety Performance'. A permanent tribute has been made to Grayson at the Nuneaton Museum & Art Gallery, and was opened in April 2009.

The Reverend Edward Milles inherited the land recorded as Newbold Comyn in Domesday together with a farmhouse that had been jointly purchased in 1539 by Richard Willes and William Morcote. He built a new house on the estate at the end of the eighteenth century and, as a great benefactor of Leamington Spa, laid out land consisting of more than 300 acres as the Newbold Pleasure Gardens for the public to enjoy.

Coventry-born Sidney Flavel (1819–1892) came from an ancient lineage whose ancestor had fought at the Battle of Agincourt in 1415. Iron founder and astute businessman, he exhibited and promoted the famous 'Kitchener' stove invented by his father William at the

Great Exhibition in 1851. It was due to Sidney Flavel's business acumen that the Flavel Company became the largest employer in Leamington for much of the nineteenth century. A commemorative blue plaque is to be found at Newbold Terrace.

Benjamin Satchwell (1732–1810) was noted for the discovery of a second spring in Leamington which led to several wells being bored and gave rise to the town becoming one of the most fashionable spas. Together with his friend William Abbott, Satchwell made the discovery of the spring and its medicinal properties on Lord Aylesford's land in 1784. He founded the Leamington Spa Charity for the sick and poor in 1806 and was the major fundraiser.

Jasper Carrott (Robert Norman Davis) was born at Acocks Green. Singer, comedian, writer of three autobiographies, games show host and star of the television series *The Detectives* with co-star Robert Powell, Jasper Carrott was awarded an OBE in 2002. He was also presented with the Lifetime Achievement Award by the British Comedy Awards on 6 December 2008.

Rugby-born actor and narrator Tim Pigott Smith, a Shakespearian thespian, is best known for the 1984 television serial *The Jewel in the Crown*.

HAVE YOU ALSO HEARD OF …

Aleister Crowley (1875–1947) was born Edward Alexander Crowley in Leamington Spa. He was also known as Frater Perdurabo and The Great Beast 666. Amongst other things he was a poet, mountaineer, chess master and author. His claim to fame was as an occultist and magician, and he has been described as the master Satanist of the twentieth century.

Sir Bernard Spilsbury (1877–1947) was from Leamington Spa. A forensic pathologist, he was instrumental in the case of Dr Crippen and the 'Brides in the Bath' murders.

A Rugby girl, Dame Rose Macaulay (1881–1958) was a novelist, critic and travel writer. Her many novels included *The Towers of Trebizond* and a travelogue, *Fabled Shore. They Were Defeated* was a study of the poet Robert Herrick and Dame Rose also produced three volumes of poetry herself. She was created Dame Commander of the Order of the British Empire in 1958.

Nehemiah Grew (1641–1712) was born in Atherstone and became a botanist and physician. His greatest work was the *Anatomy of Plants*, which is notable for its descriptions of plant structure. He was considered to be one of the pioneers of dactyloscopy and in 1684 he published accurate drawings of finger patterns.

Leamington-born composer and writer Robert Simpson (1921–97) joined the BBC in 1951. In that year he was awarded a DMus from the University of Durham. He wrote studies on the two composers who had a great influence on his work, *The Essence of Bruckner* (1966) and *Carl Nielson, Symphonist* (1979).

Economist and Nobel Prize winner for economics in 1972, Sir John Hicks (1904–89) was born in Leamington Spa.

Norman Lockyer (1836–1920) was a scientist and astronomer. He is credited with discovering helium gas along with French scientist, Pierre Janssen. He was the founder of the general science journal *Nature* in 1869 and eventually became director of the Solar Physic Observatory in Kensington, London. Lockyer was born in Rugby.

Richard Jago (1715–81) born at Beaudesert Rectory near Henley-in-Arden was a poet best known for his poem 'The Blackbirds'. He followed his father into the priesthood and was ordained to the curacy of Snitterfield in 1737.

Michael Drayton (1563–1631) was a Renaissance poet and playwright born at Hartshill. In seventeenth-century estimates of literary stature he is said to rank only slightly below the eminent poet and writer Sir Philip Sidney. A memorial bus shelter at Hartshill was erected to commemorate him. Poet Laureate Sir John Betjeman dedicated the memorial, quoting from Drayton's poem 'A Fine Day'. Drayton is buried at Westminster Abbey.

Thomas Henry Kendall, born in Kineton in 1837, was a notable woodcarver with premises in Chapel Street, Warwick. Among his many accomplishments, Kendall built a new staircase at Warwick Castle, which was destroyed in the fire of 1871. In 1872 he also carved thirty-two panels for the dining room in the House of Commons. The Warwick mayoral chain made in 1885 was from a design by Thomas Kendall. Other carvings included the choir stalls at the Lord Leycester Hospital and the pulpit at St Mary's church.

The Reverend James Harvey Bloom, rector at Whitchurch near Stratford-upon-Avon from 1895–1917, was a colourful character and something of a ladies' man. A prolific writer and antiquarian, his books included *Shakespeare's Church* and *Shakespeare's Garden*.

Ursula Bloom (1892–1984), daughter of J. Harvey Bloom, was a writer. She was appointed the chief crime reporter on the *Empire News* and *Sunday Dispatch* and was credited with the discovery of the whereabouts of Ethel le Neve, Dr Crippin's mistress, who had disappeared following his execution in 1910. Although also tried for murder with Crippin, Ethel was acquitted.

Mary Hodgkin (1910–94) from Foxcote, a research chemist and crystallographer, was awarded the Nobel Prize for chemistry in 1964.

Admiral Sir Edward Seymour of Kinwarton (1840–1929) was appointed commander-in-chief of the China Station in 1897. In this role Seymour was to later command an international force of 2,000 men to protect Western and Japanese citizens of Peking in the Boxer Rebellion. He was promoted to admiral in May 1901 and in September he had a personal audience with King Edward VII, who presented him with the insignia of a Knight Grand Cross of the Order of the Bath. Sir Edward Seymour was later promoted to Admiral of the Fleet and at the time of his death was the last living member of the original (1902) members of the Order of Merit.

William Gilbert (1799–1877) established the Gilbert Company in 1823 manufacturing sports equipment. He produced the early rugby balls by stitching together four pieces of leather around a freshly removed pig's bladder, which was then inflated by mouth through a clay pipe.

Solicitor and Clerk to the Justices, Matthew Holbeche Bloxham (1805–88) was an eminent antiquarian who wrote a book on Gothic architecture that was published in 1829 and ran to ten series.

Coventry-born Herbert Edward Cox (1870–1941) was an accomplished painter and tutor who took up textile design. Some of his patterns for textiles and wallpaper design now reside in the Herbert Art Gallery in Coventry. Cox and his wife later moved to Lillington in Leamington Spa where he has been recognised with a commemorative blue plaque at his home in Manor Road.

A leading provincial architect during the reign of George III, Joseph Pickford was born in Ashow in 1734. He later moved to London and Derby, becoming an eminent designer of town and country houses in the Palladium style.

Henry Beighton FRS (1687–1743) was Warwickshire's greatest mapmaker before the Ordnance Survey and is buried in the churchyard of All Saints at Chilvers Coton.

Leamingtonian Sir Terry Frost (1915–2003) was an eminent artist noted for his abstracts. During his career he worked as an assistant to sculptor Barbara Hepworth. Frost was knighted in 2000 and is commemorated with a blue plaque at Stamford Gardens, Leamington Spa.

Rugby-born David Barby (1943–2012) was an antiques expert who made regular appearances in the BBC programmes *Bargain Hunt*, *Flog It* and *Antiques Road Trip*.

Louisa Anne Ryland (1814–89) was said to be 'disappointed in love' and was prevented from marrying her one true love, Henry Smith Junior, by her father. Louisa remained single for the rest of her life but was to become a major benefactor to Birmingham, her hometown. Having inherited considerable wealth, Louisa contributed to recreation, education, worship and public health. She donated her estate in Moseley to the Corporation of Birmingham for a large public park. The park was called Cannons Hill Park as Louisa would not permit the name Ryland to be used.

NOTABLE PEOPLE WITH WARWICKSHIRE CONNECTIONS

Charles Louis Napoleon Bonaparte (later Emperor Napoleon III) lived in exile in Clarendon Square, Leamington Spa, between 1838 and 1839.

Anthony Eden was born in County Durham. He was elected Conservative MP for Warwick and Leamington in December 1923, his famous opposition being the Countess of Warwick, Frances Evelyn Maynard ('Darling Daisy'), who stood as a Labour candidate. Anthony Eden was to become Viscount Eden of Royal Leamington Spa and prime minister from 1955–57.

Neville Chamberlain, prime minister from 1937–40, was born in Edgbaston, Birmingham and attended Rugby School.

Dr Henry Jephson (1798–1878), born in Sutton-in-Ashfield, Nottinghamshire, came to Leamington Priors (later Leamington Spa) aged 20 years. He helped to promote the healing powers of the town's waters and built houses for the poor residents. To commemorate his good works, the Jephson Gardens were named after him and a temple was erected in the gardens in 1849 housing a marble statue.

J.R.R. Tolkien, author of *The Lord of the Rings* and *The Hobbit*, was born in Bloemfontein, South Africa, but came to live in Edgbaston, Birmingham, following the death of his mother. He married Edith Mary Bratt, three years his senior, on 22 March 1916 at St Mary Immaculate Catholic church in West Street, Warwick, after persuading her to convert to Catholicism.

In the 1750s the famous Italian painter Canaletto was invited to Warwick Castle by Earl Francis Greville, who commissioned him to do paintings of the castle. Canaletto produced five oil paintings and five pen drawings, which also included parts of the town.

Sir Robert Peel, twice prime minister from 1834–35 and 1841–46, was a major landowner of the hamlet of Kingsbury. Sir Robert helped to establish the concept of the modern police force whose officers became known as 'Peelers' and 'Bobbies'.

The notorious John Profumo (1915–2006), Secretary of State for War 1960–63, was involved in political scandal when he had an affair in 1963 with Christine Keeler, a prostitute. At that time Profumo was the Conservative MP for Stratford-upon-Avon.

Bristol-born comedian Russell Howard, famous for his television show *Russell Howard's Good News* and appearances on *Mock the Week*, now lives in Royal Leamington Spa.

Bradford-born J.B. Priestly came to live in Alveston near Stratford-upon-Avon with his third wife, Jacquetta Hawkes. A prolific and successful writer of fiction and non-fiction, playwright and sociologist Priestly was best known for his best-seller *The Good Companions*.

Writer, artist, prominent social thinker and philosopher John Ruskin is commemorated in Leamington Spa with a blue plaque at No. 12

Russell Terrace. He stayed here for six weeks to undergo Dr Jephson's celebrated salt water cure and wrote his only work of fiction, the fairy tale *The King of the Golden River*, which was published in December 1850.

Celebrated cricketer John Wisden, who played 187 first-class matches for Kent, Middlesex and Sussex, established his cricket equipment business in Leamington Spa in 1850. He was best known for the launch of the Wisden Cricketer's Almanack in 1864. Wisden is commemorated with a blue plaque at The Cricketer's Public House, Archery Road and a cricket ground was created nearby in 1849.

Well-known American novelist Nathaniel Hawthorne, best known for his works *The Scarlet Letter* and *Tanglewood Tales*, resided at Lansdowne Circus, Leamington Spa, for a few months in 1857 and has been commemorated with a blue plaque.

Thomas Wackrill, JP (1828–1907) became the first Mayor of Leamington Spa (from 1875–87) and is commemorated with a blue plaque in Portland Street.

Eminent architect William Thomas designed the grand neoclassical crescent, Lansdowne Circus in Leamington Spa in the 1830s. He emigrated to Toronto, Canada, in 1843. Thomas is commemorated with a blue plaque in Lansdowne Crescent.

Norfolk-born Malcolm Sayer (1916–70) was an aircraft and car designer. He joined the design team at Jaguar and went on to become Director of Design. Sayer was most noted for the design of the iconic 'E' type Jaguar in the 1960s, followed by the Jaguar XJS. He came to live in Leamington Spa where a commemorative blue plaque is to be found on his former home in Portland Place.

GOLFING CHAMPION

Jack Burns, born in 1859, was a Scottish man who came to Warwick in the 1880s and lived in Stand Street near to Warwick Common and the golf course. Jack kept the greens and also played golf professionally on the 9-hole course, which was the first golf course to be laid in Warwickshire.

In 1888 Jack returned to his native St Andrews and took part in the British Open Championship, which he won. The prize money was then £8 (around £600 in today's money).

The Warwick Golf Club now has a commemorative plaque in honour of their golf champion and an annual competition is held for the Jack Burns Trophy.

'NOT OUT'

Warwickshire cricket champion Frank Foster was born in Birmingham in 1889 and was to become a Warwickshire and England all-rounder. He first played for Warwickshire in 1908 and went on to do the Ashes tour, Australia in 1911/12.

Frank was noted for his fast-medium left-handed bowling and aggressive batting. In 1914 he hit an amazing innings of 305 against Worcester to give him a batting average of 34.

Frank injured his foot in an accident in 1915, which put paid to his cricket career.

Dennis Amiss was the first Warwickshire batsman to score 100 centuries in first-class cricket.

Howard 'Tom' Dollery was the first Warwickshire batsman to twice exceed 2,000 runs with a tally of 2,073 in 1952.

Jack Buckingham holds the top two places for stumpings in a season with 27 in 1937 and 25 in 1938.

Herbert Bainbridge, a Cambridge blue and Warwickshire captain, led them into the County Championship in 1895.

The inspiration for writer P.G. Wodehouse's butler in the tales of Jeeves and Wooster is said to be Percy Jeeves. Wodehouse was struck with the demeanour of Jeeves when he played for Warwickshire County at Cheltenham *v*. Gloucester at Cheltenham College grounds in 1913. A letter to Mr Ryder, displayed at the museum in Edgbaston, confirms that Wodehouse used Percy Jeeves as a foundation for his butler character. Jeeves' fifty-first class matches included Australia and South Africa in 1912 at Edgbaston. Described as a good all-rounder, Jeeves' cricket career was tragically cut short when he was killed in the First World War at the Battle of the Somme in 1916 aged 28 years. He had enlisted in the 15th Battalion of the Royal Warwickshire Regiment in 1914.

Brian Lara, 'The Prince' and former West Indies international cricket player, held the record for the highest individual score in first-class cricket with 501 not out for Warwickshire against Durham at Edgbaston in 1994. He was appointed an honorary member of the Order of Australia in November 2009.

Dermot Reeve OBE played for Warwickshire in 1990, during which he averaged 54, making his highest first-class score of 202 not out and making two other centuries on the way to a total of 1,412 runs. As captain in 1994 he led the county to a triple win, winning the County Championships, the AXA Equity & Law League and the Benson & Hedges Cup.

Ian Bell, an international and county cricketer for Warwickshire, was awarded the MBE in 2006 for his role in the successful Ashes campaign of 2005.

ON THE FLAT

Horse racing at Warwick Racecourse has a history reaching as far back as 1694 and has become a popular sport since the early 1700s.

The first races in Leamington Spa were held in 1834 on Easter Monday, 20 April, in two fields belonging to Mr James Gill.

The Leamington Steeple Chases were first held in 1834 at Ashorne.

A racehorse called Santa Claus, bred by Dr Frank Smorfitt at Marston, won the Derby in 1964.

The legendary Red Rum once raced over the flat in 1967.

Famous jockey Lester Piggott raced John Francome in 1985, taking first place.

In 2002 Irish jockey Tony McCoy beat Sir Gordon Richards' record of 269 winners in a season on Valfonic. Tony McCoy was voted BBC Sports Personality of the Year in 2010.

THE LEAMINGTON LICKER

Randolf Turpin won the Lonsdale Belt in 1956 and this was auctioned in November 2000, realising £23,000. Nicknamed 'The Leamington Licker' Randolf had acquired the moniker Licker in his childhood and it had stuck. Randolf lost his world title in a return match with Sugar Ray but regained it on 9 June 1953 at the White City Stadium against French middleweight champion, Charles Humez. Disappointingly, America refused to recognise this as a world title and insisted it be regarded as a European title only. In recognition of his world title, a statue of Randolf Turpin was erected in the Market Square, Warwick.

Randolf's eldest brother, Dick Turpin, became Midland Area middleweight champion on 22 May 1939 when he out-pointed Jack Milburn. At that time a colour bar was operated by the British Boxing Board of Control, which prevented Dick and his brother Jackie from competing for British boxing championship titles. This was lifted in 1947 and Dick went on to win the Lonsdale Belt twice.

BATTLING JACK

In 1947 Jackie Turpin had recorded thirty fights in addition to other sparring contests and boxing booths in between. As the busiest featherweight boxer, boxing writers gave him the title of 'Battling Jack'. In their earlier years, Jackie and younger brother Randolf sparred together as Aaron and Moses. In 1953 Jackie won his first British title and became the Midland Area champion, out-pointing Tommy Higgins. In *Battling Jack*, Jackie records his memoirs as a boxer and trainer; he writes about his service in the navy and how he and his brothers trained at Nelson's Gym in Warwick and Gwrych Castle in Wales.

Johnny Williams, heavyweight professional boxing champion in the 1940s and 1950s, claimed the British and Empire titles in 1952 when he won the fifteen-round fight with Jack Gardner.

'DEAD DOG'

Atherstone-born Andy Green (also known by the call sign 'Dead Dog'), a qualified fighter pilot on F-4 Phantom and Tornado F3 aircraft, is not only the holder of the World Land Speed Record but also the first person to break the sound barrier on land. On 25 September 1997 he beat the previous record in Black Rock Desert, USA, reaching a speed of 1,149.30km/h (714.144mph) in Thrust SSC. In October 1997 he reached 1,227.99km/h (763.035mph), the first supersonic record.

ITALIAN LEGEND

Former Blackburn Rovers player William Garbutt moved to Genoa, Italy in 1912 to manage the Genoa Club. Garbutt was to become a major success as a coach and manager, and became a legend in the annals of football in Italy. His career was interrupted by the outbreak of war and he returned to England in 1915 and enlisted in the army. After the war he returned to Genoa and spent two seasons with A.S. Roma before going on to Napoli. In 1935 Garbutt moved to Spain to manage Bilbao and then returned to Italy and Milan. After the Second World War, having spent a period of internment in Italy, the legendary hero returned to England to live with his sister-in-law in Leamington Spa before making his final home in Priory Road, Warwick.

SKY-BLUES

Face of *Match of the Day*, Jimmy Hill proved to be a tour de force in turning the fortunes of Coventry City Football Club in 1967. Coventry City, established in 1898, had originated from the Singers Football Club in 1883 and was languishing with a poor record when Jimmy Hill took over as manager. As lightweights in the football league tables in the early 1900s, they became known as the 'bantams' and this nickname was to stick until the 1960s. In 1967 they became Second Division champions and entered the top of the tables for the first time. The season of 1969–70 was to be the most successful in the club's history. The 'bantams' initially played at Highfield Road in Coventry. The introduction of the sky-blue strip for the 1962–'63 season was to give rise to Coventry City becoming known as the 'Sky-Blues' and when they played against First Division Birmingham City at St Andrew's in their new strip, they won 2–6.

After establishing the club as the 'Sky-Blues', Jimmy left the club in 1967 to concentrate on his television career but returned in 1975 as their managing director and chairman. The Sky-Blues played their last match at Highfield Road in 2005, after which they relocated to the Ricoh Arena until 2014. Following a dispute at the Ricoh Arena, the club moved to a temporary pitch at Northampton Town Sixfields but was reinstated at their home pitch in September 2014 when the dispute was resolved.

Former national manager and footballer Bobby Gould scored 40 goals in 82 league games for the Sky-Blues, helping them to win the Second Division title in 1966–67.

CYCLING CHAMP

Tommy Godwin, native of Solihull (historically part of Warwickshire), won two bronze medals at the London Olympics in 1948 in the team pursuit and kilometre time trial at Herne Hill. In 2012, when the Olympics were again held in London, Tommy carried the Olympic torch through Solihull.

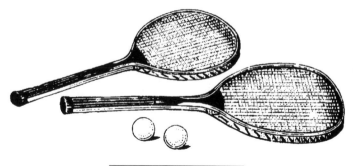

DID YOU KNOW?

The world's first lawn tennis club was founded at the Manor House Hotel, Leamington Spa, in 1872 by Major Henry Gem and Augurio Perera.

The first ladies' singles champion at Wimbledon was Maud Watson from Berkswell on 20 July 1884.

Leamington-born William Renshaw won twelve Wimbledon titles, seven of which were played in singles. He played against and also with his twin brother, Ernest. William was elected the first president of the British Lawn Tennis Association in 1888 and he and Ernest were posthumously elected to the International Tennis Hall of Fame in 1983.

Arthur Godfrey Brown was born in Bengal, India in 1915 and educated at Warwick School. A keen athlete, Brown went on to win a gold medal in the 4x400m relay in the 1936 Summer Olympics in Berlin. In 1938 he won the individual 400m at the European Championships. Brown was the headmaster of Worcester Royal Grammar School between 1950 and 1978.

Rugby player John Shurvinton was Leamington RFC's first junior international player when he played for England's Schools U-19 side in 1953–54.

World Archery Champion Naomi Folkard from Royal Leamington Spa started shooting in 1990 and achieved a silver award in the European Championships in 2008 and silver in the World Field Champions in 2010.

Nigel Murray MBE, Paralympic champion from Royal Leamington Spa, is Britain's most successful Boccia player, being a seven-time British Champion and twelve-time National Champion. Nigel won a silver medal in the individual BC2 event and the gold in the BC1/BC2 team event at the Beijing Paralympic Games in 2008. He followed this in 2009 at the European Championship in Porto, Portugal by winning a bronze in the individual BC2 event and again at the 2010 World Championships in Lisbon, winning a silver medal in the individual BC2.

Paralympic champion James Roe from Stratford-upon-Avon won a gold medal as part of the mixed coxed team in the 2012 Paralympics and was awarded an MBE in the New Year's Honours 2013.

Bedworth-based Sheila Carey was awarded the MBE in the New Year's Honours 2013 for her services to disability athletics. She was an Olympic games finalist twice – in the 1960s and 1970s in the 800m and 1,500m races.

12

THAT'S ENTERTAINMENT

SILVER SCREEN

Darlings, Luvvies
From Liverpool to Stratford was a short documentary film made
by James Fitzpatrick and directed by Ralph Donaldson in 1949.
The locations visited were the port of Liverpool, war destruction
at Coventry, historic Warwick Castle and Stratford-upon-Avon,
birthplace of William Shakespeare.

The Black Rose was filmed in 1950 at Warwick Castle. The cast
included Tyrone Power, Orson Welles, Jack Hawkins, Michael
Rennie and Cecile Aubrey.

Tom Brown's Schooldays, produced in 1951, was shot on
location at Rugby School and the cast included John Howard
Davies, Robert Newton, James Hayter, Michael Hordern and
Max Bygraves.

Prince Valiant was filmed at Warwick Castle in 1954 and starred
James Mason, Janet Leigh and Robert Wagner.

The location for *The Haunting* was Ettington Park Hotel,
Alderminster, in 1963. The cast were Julie Harris, Claire Bloom,
Richard Johnson, Russ Tamblyn and Lois Maxwell.

Candleshoe, starring David Niven, Helen Hayes and Julie Foster,
was shot at Compton Wynyates in 1977.

Death On The Nile was filmed in 1978. The cast included Peter Ustinov, Jane Birkin, Mia Farrow and Simon MacCorkindale and was filmed at Compton Wynyates.

Angels was filmed in 1995 at Arbury Hall, Nuneaton. The cast included Mark Rylance, Patsy Kensit, Jeremy Kemp, Douglas Henshall and Anna Massey.

The 2012 film *Gambit* was shot on location at Compton Verney and starred Colin Firth, Cameron Diaz, Alan Rickman and Stanley Tucci.

Lights, Camera, Action, Small Screen
Moll Flanders and *Tom Jones* were filmed at the Lord Leycester Hospital, Warwick.

In 1968 *The Expert*, starring Marius Goring, was filmed at Warwick Crown Court.

Keeping Up Appearances, starring Patricia Routledge and Clive Swift, was shot in various parts of Royal Leamington Spa in 1990–95.

In 1993 *To Play the King* was filmed at Ragley Hall, Alcester. It starred Ian Richardson, Michael Kitchen, Kitty Aldridge and Diane Fletcher.

Dangerfield, filmed in Warwick in 1995–99, starred Nigel LeVaillant and Nigel Havers.

The 1995 version of *Pride and Prejudice*, starring Colin Firth and Jennifer Ehle, included filming at the Lord Leycester Hospital, Warwick.

The 1998 production of *Vanity Fair* was filmed at Ragley Hall, Alcester. The cast included Natasha Little, Frances Grey, David Ross, Philip Glenister and Michele Dotrice.

The 1999 *Hidden Gardens*, presented by Monty Don, shows Hill Close Gardens, Warwick.

Most Haunted Live with Yvette Fielding and Paul Ross was filmed at The Falstaff Experience, Stratford-upon-Avon, in 2004.

Restoration Village was hosted by Griff Rhys Jones and featured Chedham's Yard, Wellesbourne, in 2006. Chedham's Yard won the Heritage Lottery prize money to restore the building.

In 2006 *Flog It* also came to Hill Close Gardens, Warwick, with a show presented by Paul Martin.

An episode of *Dr Who*, 'The Girl in the Fireplace', was filmed at Ragley Hall, Alcester, in 2006 and starred David Tennant and Billie Piper.

In 2007 another episode of *Dr Who*, entitled 'The Shakespeare Code', was shot at the Lord Leycester Hospital, Warwick, starring David Tennant.

The documentary series *How We Built Britain* looked at the Lord Leycester Hospital, Warwick, in 2007. The series was narrated by David Dimbleby.

Doug Strong's Special Places, presented by John Sparkes, was captured at The Falstaff Experience, Stratford-upon-Avon, in 2009.

In 2010 *The Antiques Roadshow*, presented by Fiona Bruce, was filmed at Charlecote Park.

In 2010 *Upstairs, Downstairs* was filmed in Clarendon Square, Royal Leamington Spa. Stars included Jean Marsh, Keeley Hawes, Ed Stoppard, Adrian Scarborough and Neil Jackson.

Survivors, filmed at Ragley Hall, Alcester, in 2010, starred Julie Graham, Max Beesley, Joseph Paterson, Zoe Tapper, Phillip Rhys, Chahak Patel and Robyn Addison.

The 2011 Christmas special of *Countryfile* was filmed at Charlecote Park and based around the village of Clifford Chambers. Food historian Gerard Baker demonstrated how to make a dish popular in Shakespeare's time, 'Figgy Pudding' and also a local dish, 'Coventry Cod Cakes'.

The Time Traveller's Guide to Elizabethan England, presented by Dr Ian Mortimer, was filmed at The Falstaff Experience, Stratford-upon-Avon, in 2012.

Ragley Hall, Alcester, saw the filming of *Dancing on the Edge* in 2013. The cast included Chiwetel Ejiofor, Matthew Goode, Jacqueline Bisset, Anthony Head and John Goodman.

A FLIGHT OF FANCY

Stan, the fish eagle, was demonstrating his skills during a show at Warwick Castle when he decided to make a break for freedom and flew off. The 10-year-old eagle, named Stan because he came originally from Kazakhstan, had been flying at the castle for more than eight years. He disappeared in early September 2012 and, although spotted in Northamptonshire, Stan resisted any efforts to recapture him.

On 15–21 September 1932, during a week's stopover, the County Flying Services visited a field on the Whitnash Road, Leamington Spa, with their 'Sensational Flying Display' flying circus. The attractions put on by pilots Red MacKay and Fruity Yates included wing-walker Frank Kemp walking all over the aircraft while it was being flown at 100mph and air marksmanship and bombing with big game hunters 'Colonel Popham' and 'Major Dropham'. The aircraft used were two ex-RAF Avro 504 machines.

MUSIC HALL

Ashorne Hall was once the home of the 'Nickelodeon', Graham Whitehead's collection of musical instruments and a miniature 12.25ft gauge railway with a 1-mile run. The hall was opened to the public in 1991 with its rare collection of early twentieth-century organs and musical instruments. This included two cinema organs, the Compton from the Regal in Hammersmith and the mighty Wurlitzer from the Plaza at Piccadilly Circus. The hall closed in 2003, the railway was dismantled and sold off and the collection of musical instruments was auctioned.

TO BE OR NOT TO BE

The first proper theatre in Stratford-upon-Avon was a temporary wooden building built in 1769 by actor David Garrick for his Shakespeare Jubilee celebrations to mark Shakespeare's birthday.

Brewer Charles Flower later gave several acres of riverside land to the council for a permanent memorial theatre to be erected and this was completed in 1879. This was ravaged by fire and burned down in 1926. A new theatre was built, designed by architect Elizabeth Scott, and in 1932 it was opened by the Prince of Wales, the future Edward VIII.

The Royal Shakespeare Company was formed in 1961 by Sir Peter Hall.

In Elizabethan times until 1660 only men were allowed to act and this meant that young boys would be recruited to act the part of females, often to devastating effect. They were required to wear white make-up which was lead-based and this had the unfortunate result of a high proportion of them dying from lead poisoning.

Some famous Elizabethan actors:
Edward Alleyn
Christopher Beeston
Henry Condell
William Kempe
William Shakespeare

Some famous twentieth-/twenty-first-century Shakespearian actors/ actresses:
Sir Laurence Olivier
Sir John Gielgud

Dame Judi Dench
Dame Maggie Smith
Vivien Leigh

These actors and actresses all played at the Shakespeare Theatre in Stratford-upon-Avon and many would have resided in the district for a time.

Shakespeare produced thirty-eight plays.

Four of Shakespeare's lesser-known plays:
Love's Labour Lost
All's Well that Ends Well
Timon of Athens
Titus Andronicus

Mayhem erupted in the Royal Shakespeare Theatre in 1978 when the main character walked through the audience towards the stage behaving like a drunk and shouting sexist comments. When he reached the stage he proceeded to tear down the scenery. Many of the audience fled in consternation, believing they were witnessing a real incident whereas the play, *The Taming of the Shrew*, was actually being performed as a deconstruction.

The famous actress Sarah Siddons once worked as a lady's maid for Lady Greatheed at Guy's Cliffe Manor, Warwick. She was then Sarah Kemble and married actor William Siddons in 1773. Her most notable role was as Lady Macbeth at Drury Lane, Covent Garden. William and Sarah also performed at the theatre in Theatre Street, Warwick.

A SUMPTUOUS EVENT

The 1906 Warwick Pageant, held in the castle grounds in July, was described as 'the biggest thing that had ever happened to Warwick'. The sumptuous event was produced by Louis Napoleon Parker with a cast of 2,000. A history of Warwick was depicted in twelve colourful episodes that included Elizabeth I sailing majestically up the Avon on a barge to the pageant field; Guy of Warwick with the huge Dun Cow drawn into the arena with flaming eyes; and the trial of the arrogant Piers Gaveston, Earl of Cornwall. The haughty Gaveston, richly attired in a short gold-coloured cloak with pink silk lining, white breeches, knee-length white boots with pointed toes and a chain-armour doublet,

is shown being tried by the earls. He is arraigned on spurious charges of witchcraft, theft of the king's seal, theft of Arthur's table and sacrilege.

The Kingmaker scene taken from Shakespeare's *Henry VI* produced the greatest feudal display of the day. Edward IV, asleep in his silken tent, is surprised by an angry Neville, Earl of Warwick and is taken prisoner. Neville is displeased with Edward's secret marriage to Elizabeth Woodville and is determined to supplant him on the throne with Henry VI. The Kingmaker snatches the crown from Edward's head and marches off to free Henry from imprisonment. Lady Willoughby de Broke, as Henry's wife, Queen Margaret of Anjou, appears resplendent in a white and silver brocade costume trimmed with pearls and jewels, a jewelled and pearl girdle and an embroidered purple velvet headdress complemented with a gold and pearl crown draped with a black and white veil adorning her head. She is followed by ladies of her court also dressed in elaborate costumes of the period.

The grand finale depicted Britannia, richly arrayed in white crepe with a gold cuirass embroidered with sequins and jewels, complete with a magnificent 7yd-long train. The whole gorgeously flamboyant ensemble was topped off with a golden helmet sporting a royal blue feather. Britannia carried a gold trident with the Union Jack and laurel wreath in one hand and a double-edged sword in the other. Following Britannia, six pages, also clad in white satin edged with gold, carried gold staffs bearing the name of England's colonies.

The leading parts were played by:
Mr Holte
Mr Sutton

Miss Dickens
Mr Rybot
Mr H. Brown
Mrs H. Batchelor
Mr and Mrs Sam Browne
Lord and Lady Willoughby de Broke
Lady Heath
Lady Victoria de Trafford
Reverend Ralph Goodenough

LET THEM EAT CAKE

Frances Evelyn Maynard ('Darling Daisy'), Countess of Warwick, staged a magnificent fancy dress ball at Warwick Castle in 1895 with no expense spared. The theme was based on the French court of Louis XV and XVI, and guests were asked to dress as courtiers in this period complete with wigs. The countess appeared richly attired as Marie Antoinette in a ballgown created by Jean Worth with turquoise velvet brocade embroidered with genuine gold thread in fleur-de-lys and roses. A total of 400 of Britain's high society were invited. The 'Bal Poudre' left a very sour taste with some, however. The enormous expenditure on this lavish production attracted the biting criticism of socialist Robert Blatchford in his paper *The Clarion* and he accused Frances of living a hedonistic life while the working man led a harsh impoverished existence. Stung by the criticism, Frances furiously confronted Blatchford in his office in Fleet Street, but his arguments hit home and actually led to her becoming a committed socialist afterwards.

It is reputed that Frances, 'Darling Daisy' and mistress of Edward, Prince of Wales, was the inspiration for the music hall song 'Daisy, Daisy, give me your answer do'.

ACES HIGH

A serious film buff, Charles Guy Fulke Greville, 7th Earl of Warwick, had aspirations to become a famous Hollywood actor. Adopting the stage name Michael Brooke, his big break came when he appeared in the Warner Brothers film *The Dawn Patrol* in 1938. The film, about British flying aces during the First World War, also starred Errol Flynn, Basil Rathbone and David Niven. Unfortunately the debonair earl, as his character 'Squires', failed to cut the mustard and this was to be the peak of his acting career. He gave it up shortly afterwards.

DANNY LA RUE

Female impersonator and entertainer Danny La Rue acquired Walton Hall, a nineteenth-century mansion house near Wellesbourne, in the 1970s and turned it into a country hotel. When in residence, Danny would sometimes put on improvised shows for guests. His most notable female impersonations were of Elizabeth Taylor, Zsa Zsa Gabor and Margaret Thatcher. He sold the hall in 1983.

FIRE! FIRE!

In 1992, while filming 'The Last Vampire' in the *Sherlock Holmes* series starring Jeremy Brett, Guy's Cliffe House became the scene of a real inferno. Taking place within the partial ruins, everything was set to produce a controlled fire for effect. The fire, however, suddenly flared out of control and all attempts to douse it failed. As it raged throughout the building, fire engines raced to the scene from Warwick, Leamington and Birmingham but were unable to quell it. The fire continued to burn for two days and destroyed even more of the building.

On her visit to Warwick Castle in 1572, the earl, Ambrose Dudley, had to vacate the castle with his servants and move to the nearby priory in order that Queen Elizabeth and her retinue could be accommodated. For her amusement he arranged a mock battle to take place in the Temple Fields below the castle and a fireworks display. The fireworks display went badly wrong, however, when a ball of fire set a house alight by the Great Bridge and other buildings in the town were hit. The couple occupying the house were rescued amid much hullabaloo but their house was burned down. At her command, the couple were brought before Elizabeth the next day and she gave them recompense of £25.

Following the Great Fire of Warwick in 1694, William III visited the castle on 4 November 1695. For his entertainment, a spectacular show of illuminations were created with pitch and tar and burnt on Guy's Tower while a great bonfire was lit in the courtyard. The townsfolk were also included in the celebrations and provided with 100 gallons of punch from Guy's Pot. Must have been some hangover!

In 1871 a fire broke out in Lady Warwick's dressing room at Warwick Castle and quickly spread to the east wing and Great Hall, decimating them. Although the Great Hall was gutted, a fire gap cut in the roof by firemen prevented the flames from reaching the State Rooms. Most of the treasures, such as books and pictures, were saved but serious losses were incurred in the Great Hall with the destruction of an antique marble bust of Hercules, armour and a Greek sarcophagus. As the earl, George Guy Greville, was unable to fund the restoration himself, a public restoration fund was started which raised a total of £9,651. An architect of repute, Anthony Salvin was commissioned to undertake the repairs and restoration in 1872–75.

ROLL UP, ROLL UP

Fair-goers in Rugby had an unexpected treat when they went to the Rugby Rag Fair in 1950. Elias Harris, daredevil Wall of Death rider, was accompanied by a very unusual passenger in his sidecar. Sitting serenely by his side, and evidently enjoying the ride, was a lion.

William Wombwell procured a lion called Nero and staged a fight in an enclosed arena in Factory Yard just off the Saltisford in Warwick in July 1825. The lion was set upon by three bulldogs and, although biting and disabling one dog, appeared cowed to the disgust of the onlookers. Nero had not lived up to his name or expectations. Undeterred, Wombwell decided to stage another fight on 30 July 1825 with a lion named Wallace but this time with only two bulldogs at a time.

To the great delight of the bloodthirsty crowd, Wallace demonstrated true lion aggression and put on a real wild beast show, killing both dogs. To commemorate Wallace a street was named after him but this disappeared when houses were demolished in the 1960s slum clearance.

A grave in the London Road Cemetery, Coventry, marks the tragic demise of two entertainers attached to George Wombwell's travelling menagerie. William Wombwell (nephew to George) was attacked and killed by an elephant on 12 June 1849, aged 25 years. His cousin, Ellen Blight (also known as Bright), was killed by a tiger while giving a performance as the 'Lion Queen' on 11 January 1850, aged 17 years. Ellen was accustomed to performing with the animals but on this occasion, while trying to persuade the tiger to get up, she touched it lightly with a whip. This gesture enraged the animal, which responded by crouching and then leaping at her, sinking its fangs into her chin and neck. Keepers came to her rescue and managed to extricate her from the den alive but she died minutes later.

Blood sports were a source of entertainment across Warwickshire from the sixteenth century and, although most had been banned by the mid-nineteenth century, some continued to be held. The blood sports included bear, bull and badger baiting and cockfighting and cock throwing. Cock throwing in particular continued to be held secretly in the backs of public houses and involved the bird being tethered and missiles aimed at it. The Cavalier pub in Warwick was once the scene of cockfights and a room at the back of the inn was furnished with terraced seats and a pit.

In 1900 Albert Francis Cross, poet, playwright and journalist, formed the Nuneaton Theatre and Entertainment Company and became manager of the Prince of Wales Theatre in Nuneaton.

Rock 'n' roll superstar Cliff Richards performed at Warwick Castle on 8 June 2013.

The theatre erected in Bath Street, Leamington Spa, by Mr J. Simms in 1814 was said to be particularly small. At the opening the pieces performed were *The Earl of Warwick* and *Fortune Frolics*.

In 1826, Southam Annual Fair advertised a two-day event that included Lady Godiva on horseback, St George clad in armour ready to do battle with the dragon, and bands of music to make things lively. History doesn't record whether Lady Godiva was naked on this occasion.

Leslie Clews opened a small private zoo on his farm in Southam in 1966 with a leopard and a chimpanzee among other smaller wild animals. It was later taken over by Raymond Graham-Jones, a big cat expert whose big cats were not unknown to make themselves comfortable in his home. The zoo closed in 1985.

The grand opening of the Public Hall in Windsor Street, Leamington Spa, in 1853 fell somewhat flat when Mr Warren QC stood up to make his speech. As a brilliant orator, the audience were anticipating a real treat but, in the event, the unfortunate man remained speechless; he sat down having been unable to utter a single word.

MAD JACK

For a bet 'Mad Jack' Mytton rode his mare up the grand staircase of the Bedford Hotel in Leamington Spa in 1826, out on to the balcony and jumped, whilst still seated, over the assembled diners in the restaurant below and out through a window on to the Parade.

CELEBRATIONS

The end of the Crimean War was celebrated in Warwick on 29 May 1856 with a dinner for schoolchildren and the elderly on the racecourse and a tea at the Corn Exchange.

The marriage of Edward, Prince of Wales, and Princess Alexandra of Denmark was celebrated on 10 March 1863, beginning with the booming of a cannon on Warwick Common at 11 a.m. A grand procession of the mayor and Corporation, management committee, 2,500 schoolchildren and others wended their way from the Court House to the common. The aged and adult poor were provided with dinners in their own homes and tea was given to the children at their various schools. In the evening the sky was illuminated with a big bonfire and fireworks on the hill at Warwick Common.

An interchange of young Warwick in Queensland with the old town of Warwick took place in June 1897 with the visit of the Honourable T.J. Byrnes, attorney general for Queensland and MP for Warwick, Queensland. He presented a solid silver loving cup from the mayor and aldermen of the young town to the Mayor of Warwick, then the Earl of Warwick. The cup bears the inscription: 'Presented to his Worship the Mayor and Aldermen of the Corporation of Warwick, England, by the Mayor and Aldermen of Warwick, Queensland, June 1897.'

The Earl of Warwick acknowledged this gift by sending the mayor and aldermen of Queensland a model of the famous Warwick Vase together with photographic views of Warwick.

David Warner, star of stage and screen, won the Variety Club of Great Britain award for best actor in 1966 for his performance of *Hamlet* at the Shakespeare Theatre in Stratford-upon-Avon. Leamington boy David cut his teeth as an actor in the Loft Theatre in Royal Leamington Spa.

Pailton villagers celebrated the Relief of Mafeking on Saturday, 19 May 1900 with a dance in the village hall and a special service at St Edith's church.

In 1919 the villagers of Pailton celebrated the end of the Great War with a carnival of floats and a fancy dress parade in which the children were dressed in the clothes of the nations of the world.

A world record was set at Warwick Castle on 12 September 2014 and shown on *Good Morning Britain*. The target was to become the highest number of parents and children reading from the same book at the same time for ten minutes. Author Terry Deary set 250 parents and children on their task by reading his *Measley Middle Ages* from the *Horrible Histories* series, which gained them a place in the *Guinness Book of Records*.

13

MYTHS AND LEGENDS

A DEVIL OF A DO

Meon Hill, close to Mickleton, borders on Warwickshire and
Gloucestershire. It is shrouded in mystery, said to be haunted by a
black dog and the scene of a murder attributed to witchcraft which
has never been solved. Its claim to fame is in the existence of the hill
itself. An old myth tells the story of how the Devil stood on Ilmington
Hill looking across to Evesham where the abbey was being built.
Infuriated by this sight, he gave a mighty kick, which sent a huge clod
of earth hurtling across to bury the abbey. The founder of the abbey,
St Egwin, was watching over the construction and, seeing the danger,
called upon his monks to pray with him and so avert the catastrophe.
Their prayers were answered and the clod of earth fell short of its
target, landing above the small village of Mickleton and thereby
becoming Meon Hill.

A curious tale was discovered by Thomas Kemp in *A History of
Warwick and Its People*. A soldier, Jeremiah Stone, wounded and
making his way to Warwick following the Battle of Kineton in 1642,
stayed at the Anchor while his wounds healed. He carried a bag of
money that he had pillaged from the dead bodies on the battlefield
and gave this to the innkeeper's wife for safekeeping. When he was
recovered and ready to leave he asked for his money but instead the
woman and her husband denied all knowledge of having it and threw
him out. Angrily the soldier beat on the door with his sword, trying to
break it down, until the innkeeper accused him of burglary and had
him arrested.

While the soldier languished in prison the Devil came to him and
offered to liberate him. The soldier refused, saying, 'I would rather

lose my life than my soul', and the Devil answered, 'Well, be ruled by me; when brought before the Bench ask for an attorney, choose me, by these notes thou shalt know me by a red cap and a feather.' The prisoner followed these instructions and the Devil pleaded his cause, demanding to search the house and discover the bag of money. When he heard this, the innkeeper cried out, 'I would the Devil would fetch me away now presently body and soul before you all if I swear unjustly.'

The Devil immediately 'seized upon his body and carried him away bodily over the Market Place, nothing being left behind but a terrible stink as a witness of an unclean spirit'. 'John Finch (shoemaker) in St Martin's being an eye-witness doth testify the same.'

A conical hill on the road between Stratford and Alcester is known as the Devil's Bag of Nuts. Legend says that the Devil was collecting nuts when he came upon the Virgin Mary and dropped the nuts, possibly in surprise. The 21 September is now known as the Devil's Nutting Day.

At the base of this hill a cave known as Alcock's Arbour was the den of the notorious robber, Alcock. According to legend, Alcock hid his booty in a chest secured with three locks, which was guarded by a large fierce cockerel. The chest remained hidden in the cave long after the demise of Alcock until discovered by an Oxford scholar who had found the keys. The scholar attempted to open the first lock, which yielded. He then tried the second lock, again successfully, but on his attempt to open the third lock 'the Cock seized upon him' and tore him apart. Alcock's ill-gotten gains could not be released unless, legend says, 'that of one bone of the partie who set the cock there could be brought, he would yield up the chest'.

THE LEGEND OF GUY OF GUY'S CLIFFE

When the Saxon Guy, a lowly steward, fell in love with the beautiful Lady Felice, daughter of Earl Rohund at Warwick Castle, he was determined to make himself worthy of her. To win her hand he ranged far and wide, bravely doing deeds of valour. Legend states that he slew the Dun Cow, a fearsome beast said to stand 9ft high with blazing eyes, and which terrorised and killed many villagers at Dunsmore Heath. Guy also went on to kill Colbrand, a huge 9ft giant and champion of the Danes who were besieging Winchester.

Guy won the hand of Lady Felice and after their marriage he went on a pilgrimage to the Holy Lands. On his return after many years he retired to a cave at Guy's Cliffe and lived as a hermit, doing penance for his deeds, never revealing his identity to Felice. Felice supplied him with food as alms when he presented himself at the castle as a beggar, never once recognising the gaunt figure as her husband.

When Guy felt his time was near he gave the ring Felice had given him on their wedding day to a herdsman and asked him to take it to her at the castle. On receiving the ring Felice rushed to the cave but it was too late. Heartbroken when she realised she had been giving food to her husband all along, Lady Felice leapt from the cliff into the river below and perished.

JINGLE BELLS

It is claimed by several people that the ghosts of Piers Gaveston and his captors have been seen and heard making their way up Blacklow Hill opposite Guy's Cliffe. The arrogant popinjay, Gaveston, favourite of Edward II, had risen to become the Duke of Cornwall and had made himself very unpopular with his noble contemporaries who wanted him exiled. He was eventually banished abroad but soon returned, and from then on became a wanted man. He took refuge in Scarborough Castle and surrendered to the Earl of Pembroke, who took him to Deddington near Banbury with a guarantee of his safety. However, the Earl of Warwick, who sought revenge for Gaveston calling him 'the black dog of Arden', rode to Deddington with an army and snatched Gaveston away, taking him back to Warwick Castle. Here he was put on trial, condemned and led up Blacklow Hill tied to a horse with bells. The hapless Gaveston was then beheaded in the hollow of a rock in June/July (dates vary) 1312.

In the 1990s a family of ghost hunters entered the woods on Blacklow Hill at midnight on the day Gaveston was supposed to have been executed, given as 1 July on the monument commemorating his death. They made their way, with the help of torches, to the spot where the deed was done and waited. Instead of Gaveston's ghost appearing, however, the very physical appearance of police manifested themselves in its place, having seen the torchlight and become suspicious. As the site is now on private land the red-faced trespassers had some explaining to do!

NAKED SHE RODE

Legend records that in the eleventh century, a lady rode on horseback through the streets of Coventry, naked except for her hair, which fell over her shoulders. The lady was an Anglo-Saxon noblewoman, Godiva, wife of Leofric, Earl of Mercia. Filled with sorrow for the people of Coventry who groaned under the weight of oppressive taxes imposed by her husband, Godiva begged him to be lenient and lessen their burden. Leofric agreed to do this on the condition that she rode through the streets naked and, for the sake of the people, Godiva took him at his word. A command was given that all windows should be shuttered and no one was to peek. According to legend, one person could not resist and Peeping Tom, as he became known, was struck blind.

BEAR AND RAGGED STAFF

This famous emblem of Warwick and heraldic badge of the earls of Warwick has its origin in myths of the medieval earls told by antiquarian William Dugdale in the 1650s. The bear comes from Arthgallus (Latin word *ursus*, meaning bear) who was Earl of Warwick during the time of King Arthur and who slew the bear by strangling it. The ragged staff came from Morvidus, another Earl of Warwick who reputedly tore up a young ash tree by its roots and killed a giant with it.

THINGS THAT GO CLANG IN THE NIGHT

In 1642 the Battle of Edgehill, fought between the Royalists and Parliamentarians, ended in a bloody draw with thousands dead on the battlefield. A month or so after the battle, local villagers were startled to witness two armies converging in the night sky over the battlefield and the sounds of battle raging around them, vanishing moments later into thin air.

Upon being told of this phenomenon, King Charles I despatched six of his gentlemen to investigate if the tale was true. Sure enough they too purported to have witnessed the night sky battle and had even recognised the ghost of Sir Edmund Verney, the king's standard-bearer who had been killed in the battle.

Many people claimed to have witnessed the battle scenes in the following months and years until they gradually ceased.

A London concert pianist visited the site of the Battle of Edgehill in 1960, prompted by an inexplicable urge to do so. The burial ground was then owned by the Ministry of Defence and he had to obtain permission to access it. Once this was given he set off accompanied by two soldiers. However, as he neared the burial site he began to feel unwell and was conscious of hundreds of eyes watching him. Feeling quite ill at this point and very unnerved, the pianist insisted on travelling back to London straightaway. On entering his house he became aware that he wasn't alone – one of the ghosts had accompanied him. He described the man as dressed as a Parliamentarian soldier and carrying a sword. Although offering him no harm, the continued presence caused him a great deal of alarm as he lived alone. He started to keep the lights on at night and only daylight brought him a slight relief. His continuing deterioration worried his friends who had become concerned about his health. About a month later the apparition vanished as quickly as it had manifested itself and the concert pianist made a good recovery.

THE HAUNTED TOWER

Sir Fulke Greville, owner of Warwick Castle since 1604, was brutally stabbed by his manservant, Ralph Hayward, in 1628. Although the foul deed was committed at Sir Fulke's London home in Holborn, he is said to haunt the room he used as his study in the Watergate tower at Warwick Castle. Now called the 'Ghost Tower', his murder is recreated using waxworks and special effects for the macabre entertainment of visitors to the castle.

PHANTOM BLACK HOUND

In the thirteenth century, the Earl of Warwick rewarded his elderly servant, Moll Bloxham, for her services on her retirement. On his instructions Moll was given any milk left over each day from the kitchens and allowed to sell it to the citizens of Warwick. Crafty Moll wasn't entirely satisfied with this, however, so made the milk go further by ladling out short measures. Realising that her measure wasn't entirely filling their jugs, the indignant housewives complained to the earl. Upon hearing that old Moll had abused his gift, the furious earl had her banished from the town with instructions never to come near again.

As she was being hounded out of the town, Moll cursed the earl and people of Warwick and vowed she would never leave the town. Later that night a huge black dog appeared, roaming the medieval streets. Over the nights that followed the dog visited the houses of the women that had complained and one by one they dropped dead. Afraid he would be the next victim, the earl called upon three vicars to perform an exorcism.

The exorcism was unsuccessful and Moll, in the form of the black hound, continued to roam the streets for some time. However, after the deaths of those who had been responsible for throwing her out, her malevolence dissipated and anyone coming across her in the streets at night received a dose of bad luck instead.

Meon Hill near Mickleton is also said to be haunted by a black dog. The phantom hound was seen by Charles Walton as a boy and was accompanied by a headless woman. Later that night, Walton heard that his sister had died. Much later, in 1945, Charles Walton was found murdered on Meon Hill. It is claimed that a sighting of the dog portends death.

OLD CLOTH CAP

An explosion at the Griff Colliery in September 1931 resulted in eight deaths. When the smoke cleared one of the miners was seen sitting propped up on the ground with his 'snap tin' (miner's lunchbox) beside him. Rescuers shouted to him but he didn't respond and when they moved closer it became apparent that he was dead. Investigations were carried out but were unable to ascertain the cause of the explosion, as there didn't appear to be a gas leak. When normal working life resumed, it was reported by miners that a mysterious mist appeared in the part of the shaft where the explosion had happened.

Years later a newcomer to the mines was doing the nightshift, working on his own in that part of the shaft. He was discovered in a state of collapse, unable to speak, and taken to hospital. When he had recovered he told a strange tale of seeing a mist that cleared and revealed a miner sitting propped up with his tin beside him. He described the miner as wearing a cloth cap and carrying a lamp. He shouted a greeting to the man who then rose, looked at him with piercing eyes and vanished with the mist.

When other miners heard the tale some confessed that they too had seen the figure who they had dubbed 'old cloth cap'. It was thought he was the ghost of one of the miners who had died in the blast in 1931.

'LORD HOP'

Edward Stratford, Squire of Horestone Grange, made himself very unpopular with the local residents by enclosing Horestone Fields in the mid-1700s. He also spent a great deal of time drinking in the Dun Cow and gained the nickname 'Lord Hop'. After his death, and for many years after the destruction of Horestone Grange, anyone wandering in those parts on dark nights would be terrified by the sight of the ghost of Lord Hop furiously riding around in a carriage with four phantom horses. So terrified were the local residents that the vicar of Nuneaton was asked to carry out an exorcism. The vicar managed to successfully capture the spirit of Lord Hop in a bottle and immediately pushed in a cork to prevent his escape. The bottle was then flung into a deep waterlogged pit.

Sometime later, in the early 1800s, the pit had almost completely dried out during a hot summer and someone peering into the pit spotted a mud-covered bottle. They recovered the bottle and uncorked it. There was a whooshing sound and Lord Hop was out, free to roam the neighbourhood once again.

STONE ME!

Many hundreds of years ago, when a European king came marching up from the south, close to the village of Long Compton, he was accosted by a witch at the top of a rise. Being aware that the king was ambitious, the witch said, 'Take seven long strides and if Long Compton you can see, King of England thou shalt be.' The king did as he was bid and found that he couldn't see Long Compton as his view was blocked by a hill. The witch cackled and said, 'As Long Compton you cannot see, King of England thou shalt not be.' She then turned the king and his men into stone and herself into an elder tree in the hedgerow.

The Rollright Stones on the Cotswold border with Oxfordshire are known as The King's Men, The King Stone and The Whispering Knights.

The church at Napton-on-the-Hill was originally destined to be built at the bottom of the hill and every day stones would be laid ready for construction and every night the stones would mysteriously find their way to the top of the hill, moved it was said by fairy folk. Eventually it was decided to build the church at the top of the hill where it resides to this day.

SPRING WITH A DIFFERENCE

A knight returning from the Crusades stopped to take a drink at a spring in Ettington. While kneeling to drink, the trophy he was carrying in a bag fell out into the water. The trophy was the head of a Saracen he had killed and it remained in the spring. It is said the spring never stops flowing even in times of drought.

KINWALSEY ELM

The legend of the 'Kinwalsey Elm' at Fillongley tells the tale of a couple caught stealing from the hen-roost on a neighbouring farm. The couple were subsequently tried and hanged, and afterwards their bodies were buried with a stake driven through them. The green stake took root and grew into a tree but the branches only grow out of the sides, the top being flattened as though having been hit with a mallet.

BY DESIGN

Legend has it that the eighteenth-century parish church of St John the Baptist in Honiley was designed by Sir Christopher Wren on a tablecloth. This came about when Sir Christopher dined with John Saunders, Lord of Honiley who invited him to design a church.

14

SCHEMING EARLS
AND ROMANCE

DASTARDLY DUDLEY

Robert Dudley, Earl of Leicester, had designs on Queen Elizabeth I
and wished to marry her. However, there was a problem to be dealt
with – Dudley needed to be rid of his wife, Amy Robsart, in order to
pursue his goal. On 8 September 1560, Amy was found dead at the
bottom of the stairs at her home in Cumnor by servants returning
from 'Our Lady's Fair' in Abingdon. Earlier in the day Amy had told
them all to leave the house and given her permission to attend the fair.
Rumours abounded that Dudley had had her murdered, pushed from
the top of the stairs or even poisoned (a fairly commonplace way
of committing murder in Tudor times). Nevertheless, the coroner's
verdict pointed to an accident. Amy Robsart may have been suffering
from breast cancer as she complained of 'a malady of the breasts' and
possibly depression brought about by her husband's known dalliance
with the queen and, as such, she may have committed suicide.
Although no charges were brought against Dudley, there is no doubt
he had a strong motive. In the event the scandal persisted, Elizabeth
refused to marry Dudley and he married Lettice Knollys. They had
one son who died in childhood. The effigies of all three are now in
the Beauchamp Chapel in the Collegiate church of St Mary, Warwick.

KINGMAKER/KING BREAKER

Richard Neville, Earl of Warwick, a wealthy, powerful and
charismatic lord, was at odds with certain advisors of Henry VI
and, although not wishing to actually overthrow Henry, wanted to
make him get rid of them. Initially he fought as a Lancastrian on the

side of Henry but changed sides to fight with Henry's opponent, the Yorkist Edward, Earl of March. At the Battle of Towton, the Yorkist contingent, headed by Richard Neville, routed the Lancastrians and Edward was declared King Edward IV in 1461.

Edward and Richard were great friends until Edward's marriage to Elizabeth Woodville in 1468, which caused a breach in their friendship. In 1469 the breach became openly hostile and Neville orchestrated a rebellion with Robin of Redesdale in Yorkshire. In the Battle of Edgecote, Edward found himself out-marched and out-numbered and was taken prisoner by Neville, who imprisoned him in Warwick Castle and attempted to rule in his name until protests by Parliament and the people forced Neville to release him forthwith.

In March 1470 a rebellion in Lincolnshire gave Edward the opportunity to muster an army and, anticipating retribution, Neville fled to France. Here he met up with Margaret of Anjou, the deposed Henry's wife, and together they plotted how they might restore Henry to the throne. Returning to England having managed to muster an army, Neville fought on the side of the Lancastrians once more at the Battle of Barnet in 1471. With the Lancastrian army in disarray, Neville was caught running from the battlefield and stabbed to death. On the orders of Edward IV, his body and that of his brother Montague, who had also been killed, were brought to St Paul's in London where they were displayed to the public for three days. They were eventually buried at Bisham Abbey in Berkshire.

THE FAILED PLOT

John Dudley, Earl of Warwick and Duke of Northumberland, was determined to put his niece, Lady Jane Grey on the throne following the death of Edward VI in July 1553. A successful military figure, Dudley found favour with the young King Edward as his Protector and used his influence over him to sign a document of exclusion on 21 June 1553. The document excluded Edward's sisters, Mary and Elizabeth, from succeeding to the throne on account of their illegitimacy. Edward also recorded his wish that his successor should be Lady Jane Grey. To further advance his wealth, power and status, the scheming Dudley manoeuvred the marriage of his son, Guildford, to Lady Jane, who was declared queen on 10 July 1553, reigning until 19 July 1553.

Dudley, however, had not reckoned with the will of the people, many of whom saw Mary as being the legitimate heir to the throne and, with the support of an army, Mary seized power. When Mary Tudor ascended the throne, John Dudley, with his sons Guildford, Ambrose, Robert and Henry, were seized and imprisoned in the Tower of London for treason. Also imprisoned in the tower were Lady Jane Grey and her father, the Duke of Suffolk. John Dudley was beheaded on Tower Hill on 22 August 1553 for his involvement in the plot to place Lady Jane Grey on the throne. Guildford Dudley and Lady Jane Grey were beheaded on 12 February 1554. Prior to his capture and subsequent execution on Tower Hill in 1554, Lady Jane Grey's father, the Duke of Suffolk, fled to Astley Park and hid in a great oak for three days and nights but was betrayed by his trusted manservant. Although attainted, Ambrose, Robert and Henry Dudley got away with their lives and were eventually released. Ambrose had the title of Earl of Warwick and lands restored to him and Robert became Earl of Leicester. Henry was killed at the Battle of St Quentin in 1557.

'THE BLACK DOG OF ARDEN'

Guy de Beauchamp was born in 1278 at Elmley Castle in Gloucestershire. He acquired high military renown during the reign of Edward I and distinguished himself at the Battle of Falkirk, being amply rewarded with extensive grants of land in Scotland. He was a generous benefactor to the Church, giving lands to several religious houses and also founded a chantry of priests at his manor in Elmley. Guy de Beauchamp, Earl of Warwick, was, however, to become involved in dark deeds during the reign of Edward II.

As mentioned earlier, Piers Gaveston, favourite of Edward II, was far from popular with the barons, who saw to it that he was exiled from the realm. Gaveston had humiliated the Earl of Warwick by calling him 'the black dog of Arden' and the earl swore that he would have his revenge. The opportunity to do so arose when Gaveston returned to the country as a wanted man and was captured by the earl while he was being escorted to Deddington, near Banbury.

Following a makeshift trial, Gaveston was taken to Blacklow Hill, then known as Gaveswich, near Guy's Cliffe, north-east of Warwick, and summarily beheaded in the hollow of a rock in 1312. He would have been about 28 years old. Guy de Beauchamp was careful not to be implicated in the actual execution of Gaveston. This was carried out on land belonging to the Earl of Lancaster, a powerful baron and much less likely to incur the wrath of the king. When Edward discovered his friend's death, he had his body removed to Kings Langley in Hertfordshire and buried in the Dominican priory of the Friars Preachers.

Guy de Beauchamp was to perish a few years later in 1315. It was rumoured that he had been poisoned, perhaps by the king who was outraged at the killing of his favourite. Guy was buried at Bordesley Abbey in Worcestershire. The abbey was later to fall victim to Henry VIII's Dissolution of the Monasteries. Today the ruins are in the process of being excavated.

RUTHLESS RICHARD

Richard Beauchamp (1382–1439), Earl of Warwick, was one of the richest medieval knights. He has been described as 'an avaricious knight errant with a taste for the spectacular'. He fought in the Hundred Years War for Henry V and was created Captain of Calais and also Captain of Rouen, which meant that he controlled the major crossing point between England and France together with the seat of English power in Normandy.

He was given the responsibility of overseeing the upbringing of the young Henry VI on Henry V's death and continued to lay siege to towns in France. Beauchamp's hitherto successful gains on French soil were to suffer a setback with the arrival of a young 17-year-old girl on the scene in the spring of 1429. Joan of Arc claimed that she had received divine guidance to lead an army against the English. Dressed in armour, Joan mounted a successful reversal campaign, which saw many areas recaptured by the French. The turning point came in May 1430 with the apprehension of Joan at Compiègne by John of Luxembourg.

As a valuable prisoner of war and bargaining tool commanding a hefty ransom, she was moved from prison to prison while John attempted to negotiate a good price. The ransom was eventually agreed by Richard Beauchamp and the Bishop of Beauvais. Joan was imprisoned in 1430 in the Treasury Tower of the castle at Rouen and, to ensure she did not try to commit suicide, Beauchamp had her constantly watched. He was determined to bring her to trial and oversee her execution.

The trial in February 1431 lasted five months and Joan was charged with witchcraft and heresy. The trial was suspended when she became ill, it is thought from eating carp, and Beauchamp sent his own and the king's doctors to cure her, determined that she should not die a natural death. The trial culminated with Joan being sentenced to life by the Bishop of Beauvais. The sentence enraged Beauchamp who wanted the ultimate sentence to be carried out and, while she was in prison, he ruthlessly plotted to entrap her. A bag of male clothing was left in her cell, which she then donned. Beauchamp had her interrogated and it was claimed that she had again heard voices instructing her to put on the male attire.

Brought to trial again, Joan was convicted of heresy and condemned to be burnt at the stake aged just 19 years. Beauchamp went on to achieve what he had set out to do, which was to have his young charge Henry VI crowned King of France in Paris as well as King of England.

Richard Beauchamp died at Rouen Castle on 30 April 1439, aged 57 years. In his will he left specific instructions to build a new chapel on the south side of St Mary's in Warwick to be known as the Chapel of Our Lady (now called Beauchamp Chapel).

'DARLING DAISY'

A great beauty and flirtatious, Frances Evelyn Maynard was to lead a life of extravagance and tempestuous affairs. She was to become most famous for her nine-year-long affair with Edward, Prince of Wales, later Edward VII. Queen Victoria had identified her as a possible bride for her youngest son, Prince Leopold, however, Frances was rather more smitten with the dashing Francis Greville, Lord Brooke and heir to the title Earl of Warwick. She met him at a party in 1881 when she was aged 20 and, after a whirlwind romance, they married.

In pursuance of a life of pleasure, Frances became a member of the Marlborough House Set founded by the Prince of Wales, whose members were drawn from the highest echelons of society. The Marlborough House Set devoted their lives to giving luxurious receptions and balls in grand houses in London and their country houses, and it was in these settings that Frances and the prince developed a relationship. Their romance was to continue for nine years and the prince called her 'My Darling Daisy' in his many letters to her.

After her encounter with socialist Robert Blatchford, editor of *The Clarion*, Daisy became a committed socialist. She set up her own needlework school and sought to promote technical education, which she saw as promoting social mobility to bring about a more equal society. She became increasingly concerned about the plight of the underprivileged and became involved in helping them through supporting local charities.

Daisy's affair with the prince came to an end when she was replaced in his affections by the glamorous and younger Mrs Alice Keppel but they remained friends until his death in 1910.

LADY MACBETH

Welsh actress and tragedienne, Sarah Siddons (née Kemble) was born in 1755. Daughter of Roger Kemble, who led a troupe of travelling actors, Sarah first cut her teeth on stage as a child actress. She was to become most famous for her portrayal of Lady Macbeth and appeared at Drury Lane and also at the small theatre in Theatre Street, Warwick.

As a young woman, Sarah was employed for a time as a lady's maid to Lady Greatheed at Guy's Cliffe Manor in Warwick, but was to fall for the charms of the debonair actor, William Siddons, at a tender age. In spite of strong opposition to the match from her parents (and an initial refusal for consent to marry), strong-willed Sarah was determined to get her man and eventually won the necessary consent. Aged 18 years, Sarah was married to William at Trinity church, Coventry, in November 1773.

Sarah and William had seven children but the marriage was not a happy one and the couple later parted. Tragically, Sarah outlived five of her children.

THE QUARTET

When Edward Dering, a gallant and wealthy young guardsman, fell for the charms of Rebecca Dulcibella Orpen, niece of the widowed Lady Chatterton, he approached her aunt to ask for Rebecca's hand in marriage. Lady Chatterton lived somewhat poorly at Baddesley Clinton Manor and shared it with Dering's impoverished friend, Marmion Ferrers.

Lady Chatterton, who was either very deaf or pretending to be, immediately accepted, thinking Edward was proposing to her. Although old enough to be his mother, the chivalrous young guardsman married her rather than let her down. The disappointed Rebecca formed a relationship with Marmion Ferrers and they were married in 1867.

It was decided that both couples would occupy the manor and Edward was able to furnish it with money made from writing novels. Rebecca was also a very talented artist. They lived together in perfect harmony, becoming known as the quartet. When Lady Chatterton died in 1876, followed by Rebecca's husband, Marmion in 1884, Edward Dering waited for a suitable time to elapse before proposing to Rebecca. Finally the two were united and lived out their lives contentedly until Edward's death in 1892. Rebecca lived alone in the manor until her death in 1923.

The quartet was buried in Baddesley Clinton churchyard.

15

HOSPITALS AND HYDROTHERAPY

The word hospital derives from the Latin word *hospes* meaning both host and guest. The original purpose of the *hospes* was to give shelter to strangers, particularly passing pilgrims, and these were expected to stay for one night only. Over time the medieval religious house came to provide succour for the poor and sick on a lengthier stay basis and so the seeds for the modern-day hospital were sown. Almshouses for the aged and infirm were also built to provide long-term shelter. A fine example of surviving medieval almshouses is The Guild of the Holy Cross in Stratford-upon-Avon. Originally constructed in 1269 as a hospital for poor priests of the diocese, the chapel incorporating some of the building was taken over by The Guild who built a school and almshouses in the fifteenth century.

LEPER HOSPITAL

The Leper House was designed to provide a settlement apart from society for people with leprosy and other related diseases and was located on the outskirts of a town or city. The Leper Hospital of St Michael was founded in the twelfth century by Roger de Beaumont, Earl of Warwick, and is located on a piece of land in the Saltisford, Warwick. It was governed by a warden and brethren, and small endowments were originally intended for the benefit of lepers. The chapel, which still stands although in need of restoration, allowed those being tended in the hospital to take part in religious services without infecting the wider population. A half-timbered two-storey Master's House was constructed in the fifteenth century. During the Reformation and the Dissolution of the Monasteries the hospital was given to Richard Fisher in 1535 in exchange for rent and the provision of money and four beds for the poor. *The History of Warwickshire* records that it was still in use in 1545 and provided hospitality with a weekly distribution of 8*d* and the provision of four beds for poor men in the care of a poor woman who received 8*d* per week for attending them.

Listed as an Ancient Monument, the buildings standing are considered to overlie the remains of earlier medieval buildings that included a chapel, infirmary and cemetery. The remains of the chapel and Master's House were converted to cottages in the seventeenth/eighteenth centuries. The cottages have long since been demolished and some renovation work was carried out to restore the chapel, which has again since fallen into neglect.

Today the site is in private ownership.

LUNATIC ASYLUM

The first patients were admitted to the newly built Warwick County Lunatic Asylum in 1852. This rather grim Victorian edifice occupied the land on the outskirts of Warwick at Hatton and at one point housed 1,600 patients. The asylum was virtually self-sufficient with food for the patients being provided by three farms within its grounds and water supplied from a spring. The supervising physician when it first opened was Dr John Connolly who implemented a regime of 'moral treatment', which encouraged patients to participate in both work and social activities. A rather more unpleasant treatment used well into the twentieth century was electroconvulsive therapy (ECT). Insanity wasn't the only reason for incarcerating people in these institutions; for example, unmarried mothers could be housed in the asylum.

The Warwick County Lunatic Asylum was renamed and became the Warwickshire County Mental Hospital from 1930–48. In 1948 the hospital became a part of the National Health Service (NHS) and from then on was known as The Central Hospital. As an understanding of mental health issues improved over time it was envisaged that some patients could be rehabilitated and, driven by the need to reduce severe overcrowding between the 1940s–'60s, an alternative to hospital wards was sought. Nuffield House in partnership with the Nuffield Foundation was built, providing rehabilitation units that served as a halfway house between the main hospital wards and a typical home. Although the units were supervised they were not totally controlled by staff, which allowed more freedom for patients.

The King Edward VII Memorial Sanatorium was constructed in the 1920s on land adjacent to the site of the asylum, which later became known as Hertford Hill Hospital used for the treatment of tuberculosis.

The hospital was officially closed on 31 July 1995 when it was realised that a more modern facility was needed to deal with psychiatric care and this was provided with a new purpose-built hospital (St Michael's) in Warwick. Care in the Community in the 1990s replaced the need for institutional care. Many of the old buildings at Hatton were demolished and replaced with a housing development with some of the Victorian Gothic-style buildings being retained and converted into flats.

WORKHOUSE/INFIRMARY

Warwick Hospital has its origins in the infirmary on Union Road (now Lakin Road) built in 1848. The thirty-bed infirmary was located next door to the workhouse, which catered for the poor, aged and infirm. A new hospital was constructed in 1903 and the workhouse became integrated as part of it in 1930. Conditions in the infirmary were very basic, as a commissioner's report revealed, with limited toilet facilities and chamber pots under each bed.

The Nurses Home was built in 1902 and in 1940 hut wards and medical staff quarters were erected as a result of emergency medical services required during the Second World War. The site of the proposed new District Hospital aimed at serving 200,000 patients was given the go ahead in July 1975, thereby ending six years of controversy. It was decided to redevelop the existing hospital site at Lakin Road.

It is interesting to note that, in the 1950s, visits to the children's Ear, Nose and Throat ward was limited to four days only and by special arrangements on others.

Today, Warwick Hospital is run by South Warwickshire NHS Foundation Trust and provides 350 beds and inpatient, outpatient and diagnostic services. As infectious diseases have declined due to widespread vaccination and use of antibiotics, these have been overtaken with the diseases of affluence, requiring more sophisticated and expensive treatments. The purpose-built Aylesford Unit, erected in 2008, offers cancer services to patients in South Warwickshire and was designed with significant input from patients to ensure the services reflected their needs.

In 1837 an infirmary was opened in Shipston-on-Stour as part of the workhouse. This was later renamed as Shipston House and became a geriatric hospital. The hospital was housed in a new building in the 1970s on the Darlingscote Road and renamed Low Furlong, which is now a residential care home.

WHAT'S IN A NAME?

Opened in 1948, the George Eliot Hospital in Nuneaton is a single-site hospital. In common with many buildings in the area, it was named after novelist George Eliot (Mary Ann Evans) who lived on the nearby Arbury Estate. Many of the hospital wards are named after characters in her novels, e.g. Caterina, Adam Bede and Dolly Winthrop. Originally the Manor Hospital in Nuneaton retained the Accident & Emergency Department, operating theatres and orthopaedic wards until its closure in 1993 when these facilities were transferred to the George Eliot Hospital.

The hospital is very innovative and set up its own museum as a teaching aid in 1982. However, due to cost-cutting measures, this was forced to close in *c.* 2005. Another educational tool, the George Eliot Training and Education Centre (GETEC) was opened in late 2006. This was developed to accommodate a range of education and training events for undergraduates, postgraduate professionals and support staff to help drive forward the Trust's vision to encourage lifelong learning in the National Health Service. Funding for the centre was made available through resources specifically set aside for teaching by the Department of Health and former West Midlands South Strategic Health Authority.

The George Eliot NHS Trust Hospital has 352 beds and serves a population of 29,000 drawn from Nuneaton and Bedworth, north Warwickshire, south-west Leicestershire and north Coventry.

ISOLATION HOSPITAL

Originally used as a 'fever' or isolation hospital, the Heathcote Hospital in Leamington Spa was first opened in 1858. The hospital treated all types of infectious diseases, including tuberculosis and scarlet fever. Patients were kept segregated from the wider community until they were deemed no longer infectious. This continued for over ninety years, after which Heathcote Hospital became a chest hospital in 1950 and a rehabilitation hospital for the elderly in 1958.

The Royal Leamington Spa Rehabilitation Hospital, as it is now called, has three wards, Arden, Campion and the state-of-the-art Feldon Stroke Unit, which was formally opened on 6 June 2006. There is also a Day Unit, which provides outpatient, physiotherapy and occupational therapy in addition to other medical services.

PHANTOM HOSPITAL

The Lord Leycester Hospital in Warwick was founded by Robert Dudley, Earl of Leicester, in 1571 for the charity of twelve poor brethren (old soldiers). The word 'hospital' is something of a misnomer in this instance as it has never been a hospital in the modern-day sense; the term is instead used in its ancient sense to mean 'a charitable institution for the housing and maintenance of the needy, aged and infirm'.

Today the medieval buildings serve as a retirement home for ex-servicemen and their wives. These are still collectively known as the 'brethren' and wear on special occasions the traditional black gown and Tudor hat adorned with the silver crest of the bear and ragged staff, emblem of the earls of Warwick. In addition to providing a retirement home, the Lord Leycester Hospital is also a major tourist attraction in Warwick.

PRIVATE HOSPITAL

As an alternative to NHS-run hospitals, a private hospital at Blackdown, Leamington Spa, was established in 1981 as a charitable trust and joined the Nuffield Health Hospitals in 1994. The Nuffield Health Warwickshire Hospital offers the latest facilities and technology for the care of patients with a range of surgical and medical requirements and serves the Coventry and Warwickshire regions.

HOSPITAL DECEASED

The Warneford Hospital on Radford Road, Leamington Spa, named after Dr Samuel Warneford, was established in 1832. Dr Warneford stayed in Leamington Spa in 1831 during which time he had hydrotherapy treatment at the spa baths and, as a result, decided to have a hospital built in the town, which he wanted to make good use of hydrotherapy.

From 1869 until 1948 it became known as Warneford Leamington & South Warwickshire General Hospital, after which it was Warneford General Hospital until 1981 and then Warneford Hospital until its closure in the early 1990s.

Many children from Leamington Spa and its surrounds were born in Cay Block, the maternity ward. Cay Block was opened in 1939 and named after Mrs Annie Cay from Kenilworth, who was a fundraiser for the hospital and a benefactor. She donated £1,000 at its outset and a further £1,000 on completion.

In an article 'Remembering the Warneford' in the *District Advertiser*, Irene Cardell highlights the terms and conditions patients underwent to gain access to the hospital prior to the implementation of the National Health Service. With no National Health Service to cover the cost of patient care the hospital depended on voluntary contributions and these were made through donors and regular subscribers. These included the wealthy, such as the Earl of Warwick and Lords Dormer, Leigh and Percy, businesses like Burges & Colbourne and Nelson & Company and also friendly societies such as Oddfellows. Instead of patients being referred by a doctor, access to the hospital was by means of a ticket obtained from a donor or subscriber. Those applying for tickets were more likely to be favoured if they were clean and respectable. On no account was anyone suffering from an infectious disease admitted.

Much of the treatment carried out at the Warneford Hospital was hydrotherapy. Provision was also made to treat wounded soldiers from the Boer War and First and Second World Wars.

Closure of the Warneford Hospital was brought about by the need to centralise services in one location rather than have them based in three small general hospitals in Warwick, Leamington Spa and Stratford-upon-Avon. A site was determined for a more comprehensive hospital in Lakin Road, Warwick.

COTTAGE HOSPITAL

The Ellen Badger Cottage Hospital in Shipston-on-Stour was founded on 22 September 1896, the main benefactor being Richard Badger who financed the building and furnishings as a memorial to his wife, Ellen. The hospital was designed by his childhood friend, Edward Mountford, and supported with voluntary contributions.

The hospital gradually expanded over the years with the number of beds increasing from five to thirty-five. A maternity unit of eight beds was provided in 1934 until 1973. Today there are nineteen inpatient beds, an X-ray department, physiotherapy and occupational therapy facilities, chiropody and consultants' clinics and a daytime minor injuries facility.

A new Day Unit was opened in 1992 by the Princess of Wales and a horticultural therapy garden added in May 2004.

Today the Ellen Badger Hospital, as it has been known since 1922, is a community hospital supported by The League of Friends of Shipston-on-Stour who also support Low Furlong Residential Care Home. The League was established in March 1973 as a registered charity.

HYDROTHERAPY

Hydrotherapy was first introduced in Britain in 1842 by Captain R.T. Claridge and involves the use of water for pain relief and treatment through occupational therapy and physiotherapy. Complaints treated include arthritis, gout, skin disorders and, more recently, colonic hydrotherapy. Various therapies used in hydrotherapy employed water jets, underwater massage, mineral baths, hot tub and cold plunge. Treatment worked by stimulating muscles and circulation, soothing muscles or increasing the metabolism. Before the Second World War, forms of hydrotherapy were also used to treat alcoholism. The specific use of heat was associated with the Turkish bath and this was introduced with a swimming bath in 1863 at the Royal Pump Rooms in Leamington.

The Royal Pump Rooms and Baths were first opened in 1814 in Leamington Priors, a then small village. It included the world's first gravity-fed piped hot water system. A notable visitor to the baths was Napoleon III who stayed in Leamington from 1838–39.

From the 1840s the growing popularity of hydrotherapy, which used pure water rather than mineral-rich waters, came under threat with the rise of seaside and foreign resorts. By 1860 all except one of the bath houses in Leamington had closed down.

Dr Henry Jephson, a physician who practiced in Leamington Spa, was attributed with promoting the expansion of the town as a health spa in the early nineteenth century and later commemorated with a marble statue and gardens named after him. Dr Jephson helped to save the Royal Pump Rooms from closure in 1861 when he persuaded forty-one local people to form a consortium to buy the building. They carried out a series of renovations to try and attract more visitors.

Charles Ravenhill and William Leist were managers of the Royal Pump Rooms in the first half of the twentieth century and during this time both fresh and saline waters were used. They implemented schemes to refurbish the Royal Pump Rooms and introduced new treatments to keep up with changing fashions in bathing and by 1926 a number of new and updated facilities had opened.

Vortex baths were first installed in 1949 and were frequently used until 1990. The vortex bath for private patients in the 1980s cost £2.50. The Therapeutic Pool was, by the 1970s, increasingly used to treat patients recovering from road accidents.

Since 1948, physiotherapy and hydrotherapy treatments had been available under the National Health Service but patients could still pay for private treatment at the Royal Pump Rooms although the majority were referred by a NHS consultant.

The Turkish bath and slipper baths closed in the mid-1970s, the swimming pool closed in 1989 and the hydrotherapy and physiotherapy departments closed in 1990.

The Royal Pump Rooms were closed in 1997 for redevelopment by the District Council and reopened in 1999 as a culture centre.

SELECT BIBLIOGRAPHY

Anand, Sushila, *Daisy: The Life and Loves of the Countess of Warwick* (Piatkus, 2009)

Bourne, Roy, *A History of the People of Pailton, Warwickshire* (Bourne, 1984)

Carvell, Steve, *Twentieth-Century Defences in Warwickshire* (The History Press, 2007)

Copson, Pamela (ed.), *The Warwickshire Countryside: An Ecological Evaluation* (Warwick Museum, 1980)

Dugdale, William, *Antiquities of Warwickshire* (London: Thomas Warren, 1656)

Edgerton, Paul, *William Garbutt: The Father of Italian Football* (Sportsbooks, 2009)

Faulkner, Alan H., *The Warwick Canals* (Railway & Canal Historical Society, 1986)

Field, Jean, *Kings of Warwick* (Brewin Books, 1995)

Field, Jean, *Rangemaster of Royal Leamington Spa 1777–2005* (Brewin Books, 2006)

Goodwin, W.T., *Warwick Baptist Church* (self-published, n.d.)

Griffin, Alan, *Leamington's Czech Patriots and the Heydrich Assassination* (Feldon Books, 2004)

Halford, Brian, *The Real Jeeves: The Cricketer Who Gave His Life for His Country and His Name to a Legend* (Pitch Publishing Ltd, 2013)

Hancock, David, *Historic Pubs & Inns of Warwickshire* (Countryside Books, 1995)

Harkin, Trevor, *Coventry April 1941: The Forgotten Air Raids, Awards and Accounts* (War Memorial Park Publications, 2011)

Hawke, Dee, *Memories of Warwick Crown Court* (self-published, n.d.)

Kemp, Thomas, *A History of Warwick and its People* (H.T. Cooke & Son, 1905)

Manning, J.C., *Glimpses of Our Local Past* (C. Forster, 1991)

Maynard, Evelyn, Countess of Warwick, *Warwick Castle and its Earls: From Saxon Times to the Present Day* (Hutchinson & Co., 1903)

Palmer, Roy, *The Folklore of Warwickshire* (Llanerch Press, 1994)

Shill, Ray, *Birmingham's Industrial Heritage 1900–2000* (Sutton Publishing, 2003)

Spinks, Philip, *Brooke's Battery* (Brewin Books, 2008)

Sutherland, Graham, *Warwickshire Crimes and Criminals* (Knowle Villa Books, 2008)

Tennant, Philip, T*he Civil War in Stratford-upon-Avon: Conflict and Community in South Warwickshire, 1642–46* (Sutton Publishing, 1996)

Turpin, Jackie and W. Terry Fox, *Battling Jack: You Gotta Fight Back* (Mainstream Publishing, 2005)

Veasey, E.A., *Nuneaton in the Making: Industrial Growth* (Jones-Sands, 1984)

ABOUT THE AUTHOR

LYNNE R. WILLIAMS is a well-travelled local history enthusiast. She has a degree in social studies and is the author of *Warwick Then & Now*. Now retired, Lynne spends her time researching history. She lives in Warwick.

Also from The History Press

WARWICKSHIRE

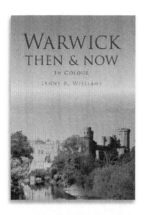

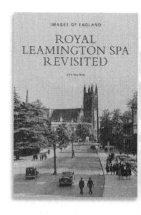

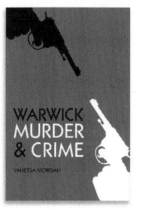

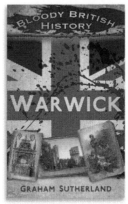

Find these titles and more at
www.thehistorypress.co.uk

Also from The History Press

MURDER & CRIME

This series brings together numerous murderous tales from history. Featuring cases of infanticide, drowning, shooting and stabbing, amongst many other chilling killings, these well-illustrated and enthralling books will appeal to everyone interested in true crime and the shadier side of their hometown's past.

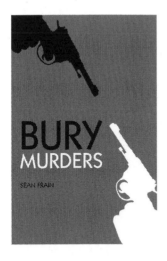

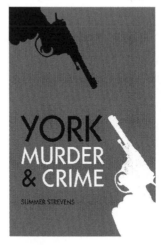

Find these titles and more at
www.thehistorypress.co.uk

Also from The History Press

HAUNTED

This series is sure to petrify everyone interested in the ghostly history of their hometown. Containing a terrifying collection of spine-chilling tales, from spooky sightings in pubs and theatres to paranormal investigations in cinemas and private homes, each book in the series is guaranteed to appeal to both serious ghost hunters and those who simply fancy a fright.

Find these titles and more at
www.thehistorypress.co.uk

Also from The History Press

WHEN DISASTER STRIKES

Also from The History Press

ᛘᛁᚳᛏᛟᚱᛁᚨᚾ ᛘᛁᛚᛚᚨᛁᚾᛋ
VICTORIAN VILLAINS

Find these titles and more at
www.thehistorypress.co.uk

Made in the USA
Middletown, DE
07 December 2021

54559563R00108